DYNASTY

DYNASTY

Building a Championship Insurance Team

Chase Gruening and Emily Gruening

©2025 All Rights Reserved. No portion of this book may be reproduced, stored in a retrieval system, or transmitted in any form or by any means—electronic, mechanical, photocopy, recording, scanning, or other—except for brief quotations in critical reviews or articles without the prior permission of the author.

Published by Game Changer Publishing

Paperback ISBN: 978-1-968250-14-0

Hardcover ISBN: 978-1-968250-15-7

Digital ISBN: 978-1-968250-16-4

www.GameChangerPublishing.com

For Remi and Hunter—

You are our why.

May you always know the power of belief, the strength of showing up, and the legacy that's built one play at a time. Never let anyone— or anything—tell you that you can't or that you won't.

This isn't just our story. It's the foundation for yours. Keep your head high, your heart strong, and your feet moving forward.

*We're in your corner. Always.
Love,
Dad & Mom*

BECOME A CHAMPIONSHIP PRODUCER
BUILD A CHAMPIONSHIP TEAM

Scan the QR Code:

DYNASTY
BUILDING A CHAMPIONSHIP INSURANCE TEAM

CHASE GRUENING AND EMILY GRUENING

FOREWORD

BY AARON KUNZ, ILLINOIS STATE CHAMPION HEAD FOOTBALL COACH, WILLIAMSVILLE HIGH SCHOOL

Chase Gruening first stepped onto the football field at Williamsville High School in the fall of 2003—the same year I took over as head coach. He was a freshman defensive lineman; I was a first-year head coach, replacing Illinois High School Football Coaches Association Hall of Famer, Paul Jenkins. The program had experienced great years since its start in 1972, but my previous four years as an assistant coach had been marked by just 14 total wins. Our first season together as head coach and player was even more challenging—we went 1-8.

But that tough season planted the seeds of something special. Chase played on a JV team that went 7-1, and over the next three years, he became an integral part of the program's turnaround. Over the next three years as an offensive and defensive lineman, he helped lead us to 23 wins, multiple playoff appearances, and our first IHSA playoff victory since 1995.

Chase was a relentless competitor—driven in the weight room, intense on the field, and completely selfless. He was the kind of player who would do anything for his teammates. His impact was felt not only in wins and accolades—including multiple All-Conference selections and a spot on the Illinois High School Football Coaches Association All-State Team—but in the culture he helped build a culture of loyalty, effort, and accountability.

He carried those same traits into college, where he was a four-year starter at Millikin University and later began coaching at the collegiate level, including a MAC championship season at Northern Illinois University in 2014. But even with success, Chase came to a realization—college coaching wasn't the life he wanted long-term. And in a bold move, he transitioned to a field that would ultimately become his passion: insurance.

Chase's story in insurance started humbly—knocking on doors, selling policies one client at a time. Around the same time, in 2016, he returned to coach alongside me at Williamsville, leading our special teams for three seasons. It was a full-circle moment—now not as coach and player, but as colleagues and friends. He brought energy, accountability, and leadership to our program once again, this time from the sidelines. Our bond deepened as we shared both success on the field and the joys of watching his business take shape.

Those years were a turning point in Chase's life. He launched the Chase Gruening Agency, began laying the foundation for what would eventually become Gruening Health and Wealth, and—most importantly—met Emily Lauritson on a trip to Nashville. She quickly became the love of his life, and her influence on Chase—personally and professionally—was profound. He moved to Tennessee, expanded his vision, and together they started building something special.

Today, Gruening Health and Wealth is a rapidly growing agency focused on serving Medicare and retirement clients.

But Chase's passion for coaching never left.

FOREWORD

In 2021, Chase and Emily launched COACHG—a coaching and training company built to develop the next generation of elite insurance agents and agency leaders. What started with a handful of agents quickly evolved into a national movement, offering programs, masterminds, and performance coaching grounded in the same championship principles that shaped his football career.

Through COACHG, Chase came full circle: back to coaching—only now, the playbook builds businesses. From Top 5 "Best of Springfield" honors to top producer awards, Chase has become not just a successful businessman, but a builder of people.

Along the way, he's also built a great life at home. Chase is a dedicated husband to Emily and a proud father to their daughters, Remi and Hunter. It's been fun to see him not only grow as a coach and businessman, but also as a family man—his greatest and most important team.

From that first snap in 2003 to the pages of this book, I've had a front-row seat to Chase's journey—from player to coach, coach to entrepreneur, and teammate to visionary. In *Dynasty: Building a Championship Insurance Team*, Chase shares the leadership principles, lessons, and culture-building insights that helped him become the CEO and innovator he is today.

For those looking to lead, grow, and build something great—whether in sports, business, or life—this book is for you.

CONTENTS

Introduction   xv

SECTION 1: BECOMING A CHAMPIONSHIP PRODUCER

1. Draft the Right Team   9
2. Run the Right Route   17
3. Agent of Interest   21
4. Fill the Stands   29
5. Reps Win Games   35
6. Watch the Film   41
7. ME to WE   47
   - Section 1: Conclusion   53

SECTION 2: BUILDING A CHAMPIONSHIP TEAM

1. Build the Brand, Build the Buzz   61
2. Protect the Locker Room   73
3. Lead From the Front   81
4. Practice Like You Play   89
5. Tighten the Playbook   97
6. Call the Perfect Play   103
7. Win the Fans   109
8. Keep Score Like a Pro   117
9. Scale the Roster   125
10. Make the Adjustments   133
11. Leave a Legacy   139
12. The Plays I'd Call Differently   145

Conclusion: The Dynasty Mindset   151

INTRODUCTION

I truly believe that our past shapes us—and that we are most qualified to lead who we once were.

It's funny, because I've spoken at a lot of events and often skip straight to my 20s when I share my story. That was the "cool" part of my life and what a lot of people know me for—transitioning from college football coaching to building a multi-million-dollar insurance agency. It was the comfortable part of my past, and it was easy to share.

Sure, football will always be the core of my story and a major part of who I am. But what most people don't know is that football replaced my father. My father was virtually non-existent growing up. I really only have two memories of him from my teenage years. The first, oddly, is one I'm not even sure is real—it's just one that sticks in my mind. I was in the middle of a JV football game my freshman year, and I looked over between plays. There was my father, leaning against the sideline fence, watching me play. It's one of the only memories I have of him being there for me.

INTRODUCTION

The next memory is from when I was around 19 or 20. I knew my dad worked at Sears, the old department store. My then-girlfriend and I decided it would be fun to walk through Sears on our way to the mall to see if we could spot him. I remember walking down the main aisle toward the mall, and I glanced over at the lawn-mowers—because I'd been told my father worked in Lawn and Garden and sold them. He wasn't there. I turned my eyes back to the aisle—and there he was, walking toward me. We looked each other up and down as we got closer. A few feet apart, I stopped and smiled. I'll never forget him saying, "Do I know you?"

I didn't really react, though my girlfriend was visibly upset. I told him, "Yes—I'm your son."

He quickly tried to recover and said, "Oh yeah, I thought that was you."

Looking back, I realize I was pretty numb to the situation. I think, subconsciously, I always knew that my father was never really there—and never really knew who I was.

I don't want to dwell on this too much, because although my father wasn't there for me, football always was. And I had some incredible male role models growing up—my best friend Tyler Sloan's father, Uncle Mike; Coach Aaron Kunz, my high school football coach, who's now one of my best friends and was a groomsman in my wedding; and Scott Sheff Sr., who would do anything for me. These are just a few of the men who helped shape me, along with the sport of football.

Football was everything to me growing up. I dedicated myself to the sport, my teammates, and my coaches. I was an all-state high school football player, a captain, and eventually went on to play college football. I often tell people I didn't go to college for school—I went to play football. And that's the truth. It's no surprise that the same story continued in college. I was an all-conference player, a captain, a leader—someone my coaches and

INTRODUCTION

teammates could always count on. Football, my teammates, and my coaches were always there for me.

Eventually, football ended in my senior year of college. I graduated with a four-year degree in fitness and sport—and was quickly left to discover that I had no clue what I wanted to do with my life. That was a really crappy feeling: to spend thousands of dollars, go into debt to play football, and still not know what to do with the rest of my life. I know a lot of people have been in the same place: at a standstill, wondering, *What the heck am I supposed to do???*

For me, I just turned to the only thing I knew—football. I decided to go into coaching professionally at the collegiate level and spent one season at my alma mater as an intern before my journey across the country began as a college football coach. Just like when I played, I wanted to win, and I wanted to climb the ladder to Division I. So I did just that. I was at four schools in four years and eventually ended up at NIU—a non–Power 5 Division I school in the MAC conference. We won a conference championship that year and got a big, fat championship ring. From the outside looking in, I was living the dream as a big-time college football coach.

What people didn't see? I was actually an intern at that level, sleeping on a pull-out couch and making $2,000 that year. I lived on handouts, and my quality of life was at an all-time low. Even worse, the head coach was a complete asshole. Coaching at the college level is just like business. The head coach—AKA the boss—has a huge impact on the culture and your quality of life. He was simply a poor leader of people, and of men in general. That was the beginning of me questioning whether this was the life I wanted. I went back to my alma mater as a full-time coach, making $28,000. Honestly, the quality of life was great—but our team was terrible. We won two games. And as they say in coach-

INTRODUCTION

ing, there are two types of coaches: those waiting to be hired and those waiting to be fired. You can guess the rest: we got fired.

The thing is, I knew we were going to get fired. I had already decided, as the season wrapped up, that I was going to make the tough transition to selling Medicare insurance with my college roommate, Luke Hockaday, at Sams/Hockaday & Associates—a small captive shop in Decatur, IL. When I say this was tough, I mean *TOUGH*. I felt like I had wasted six years of my life, and honestly, I felt like I was giving up—which was something I had never done before. I actually moved back into my mother's basement to save money, since I was taking a 100% commission job. It was a crappy place to be. But I thought, *Hell, I was able to convince top recruits to pay $30K a year for college to play football—I can sell insurance. That's something people actually want and need.*

Overall, I just felt like it was the right move for me. And the guys I worked for lived a beautiful life. I wanted that—for myself and my future family. The silver lining at the time was that I was able to coach at my high school as a volunteer, for free—which I didn't know then would turn out to be the best coaching years of my life.

With all that being said, I did the only thing I knew: I worked my butt off. I quickly became the top agent at the agency, and people started to take notice. I was knocking on doors like a madman and selling a crazy amount of policies for a new agent. People outside the agency began asking questions—like, "Have you thought about starting your own business?" or "Why not do this on your own?" The truth is, I remember selling LEGOS growing up, or running garage sales as a kid. I have always loved making money and selling things. And the thought of owning my own business started becoming a daily one. So, about 15 months into selling insurance, I left the firm I was with and started my own practice: Chase Gruening Agency.

INTRODUCTION

It was at this point in my life that I felt somewhat alone for the first time. I had left the agency I was working for, and they weren't overly happy about it—it took some time to heal. I was always used to being part of a team: feeding off others, competing with others, and ultimately leading others. But again, I just put my head down and worked. I had a lot of success and thought this was what my life would look like. I'd make a couple hundred thousand dollars a year—maybe half a million—and live a pretty good life when it was all said and done.

I wasn't totally alone, though. My mother, Tamara, came out of retirement to help me start the business—something I'll always be grateful for. She has truly supported me in every success and failure I have ever encountered. After about two or three years of doing my own thing, a couple of guys showed up: Travis Goveia and Jack Hockaday. Both were former college football players. Travis was actually a player I coached at Millikin University, and Jack is the brother of Luke—the one who got me into the business in the first place. These guys don't know it, but they really changed my life. Without them seeking me out and taking a chance, I don't think we'd be where we are today as a company. And I don't think I would've had a reason to do and be more. These guys gave me the passion to lead and coach again. They helped me see that my ten years of coaching high school and college football weren't for nothing. I was finally leading my own team. I was the head coach. That's when I realized I had intentions of this being much bigger than me. And my now wife, Emily—who you'll meet later in the book—played a major role in helping me rebrand to Gruening Health and Wealth.

It was really just the three of us for a couple of years. Travis and Jack were having minor success, and as a leader and coach, I knew they needed more. I met a couple of key individuals—Justin Thomas Falck being one—who helped me implement a

INTRODUCTION

marketing system that solved a lot of problems in our business. We literally had everything except consistent lead flow. Our internal sales and systems were so freaking optimized—we were selling insurance like hotcakes when we had a lead—we just needed more people. We needed to amplify what we had, and Justin gave us just that.

We quickly exploded. I was already in the process of buying an office, and agents started showing up—go figure, they were almost all athletes. You'll hear me talk more about this throughout the book, but what happened next was absolutely incredible. We scaled, and we scaled fast. We went from three agents in 2022 to 500 + agents in 2025.

We now have a true championship team and culture.

Throughout this book, you're going to hear me talk a lot about **Optimize, Amplify, Scale.** It's a major part of what we teach, preach, and coach. And yes, I know how to help you do all those things very well. It's what most people come to me for now—to help them grow their business and make money.

But what I'm most proud of is the culture, team, and community we've built. I know what it's like to feel alone in both life and business. Football taught me everything about building a championship insurance team—what I call a dynasty. Something that will live long after me and my family. I always say it's just like that, only different. I still coach and lead people every day of my life; it's just in the sport of insurance. I don't know any other way than showing up for people. It's who I am. My promise to you: if you show up for me, I will show up for you—and I will not let you lose.

Thank you for showing up. Let's get started.

SECTION 1: BECOMING A CHAMPIONSHIP PRODUCER

A lot of people put the cart before the horse. Many of the people I meet want to build a championship team or grow something really big. The most important thing people need to realize is this: you have to be a championship producer before you can build a championship team.

In my opinion, that's the foundational step on the ladder—becoming a championship producer. Over the last decade of building a team and being a championship producer myself, I really feel like I've found a formula that helps you do just that and lays the groundwork for everything else. So, if you're brand new to the insurance industry, getting into it for the first time, or you're a struggling agent working on your own, I think it's crucial to understand that becoming a championship producer at a high level will enable you to eventually teach it to others.

One thing I've always been told is this: you're most qualified to teach who you once were. And for those of you reading this who are struggling agents or just trying to get to the next level—that's who I once was. I was a struggling agent. I was a solo agent. I started this operation in my mother's basement. I made $33,000 my first year in insurance. Before that, I was sleeping on couches. So, I know what it's like to be at the lowest lows—and I also know what it's like to reach the highest highs.

Really, the way I've written this book is for the person I once was—helping that person expedite their future. When it comes to becoming a championship producer, I think the most important thing you can do is find a mentor or a community. For me, I've always been a sports guy, as I've alluded to, and I've always been fortunate to have that mentorship or community around me.

One of my biggest mentors was Coach Aaron Kunz, my high school football coach. He's actually one of my best friends now—he was in my wedding. But back then, from age 14 to 18, he was a mentor who made a major impact on my life. That mentorship shaped me going into college and ultimately helped me make some crucial decisions—like getting into the insurance industry when I thought my life was going to be all about football.

That was a personal mentor. When I transitioned into the insurance world, I went to work for Sams/Hockaday, which was an LOA shop. For those who don't know what that is, LOA means I was captive—they owned my commissions. I had a contract with them that essentially made me an employee. And that's fine. Honestly, I think anyone who's brand new should spend at least their first year working under someone with deep mentorship—shadowing and learning from someone who's performed at a high level. In my opinion, that's what will separate you from the start: finding a mentor or plugging into a successful community. Luke Hockaday, the son of the owner and my college roommate, was a big part of that journey.

Luke's one of my best friends. He was also in my wedding. As you'll see throughout this book, a lot of people were in my wedding, and Luke was one of them. At the time, I was coaching football and moving all over the country. He said to me, "Man, you're getting kids to pay $30,000 to $35,000 a year for school. You should sell insurance. It's a lot easier, it's a lot cheaper, and people actually need it."

I said, "Okay, maybe someday."

Well, fast forward—and that's eventually how I got into insurance. It just made sense for me at the time.

I loved the idea of competing and being in charge of my own income and future. So I transitioned into Sams/Hockaday, and my real mentor there was Michael Sams, the son of the other owner, Jeff Sams. I learned under Michael for about 15 or 16 months. He was an incredible producer—operating at a high level, a great teacher, and a great coach. Our personal lives are very different—Michael and I—but I respect him deeply for that. Professionally, he laid the groundwork for everything for me. I took a lot from him, developed some of my own methods, and he's still a world-class producer to this day.

We compete—we've got a friendly rivalry from afar—but without that mentorship, without those 15 months of deep work under someone who had really demonstrated success at a high level, I don't think I'd be where I am today. So, when it comes to the insurance side, I attribute a lot of my early success to Michael Sams, Luke Hockaday, and the Hockaday and Sams families. I'll forever appreciate them. Fast forward eight or nine years later, and now you'll hear me talk a lot about Coach Micheal Burt. He's been a phenomenal mentor and an incredible leader.

One thing I always say is: mentors and leaders—those kinds of people—come in and out of your life at different times for different reasons. For me, when I knew I wanted to develop a coaching program, a community, a world-class space where insurance agents could train, grow, and reach new heights, I turned to

Coach Micheal Burt. He had already built an eight-figure coaching business and had done it at a high level.

I always look for "the who"—who has done what you're trying to do? Go find a "who" who can teach you "how." You'll hear me talk a lot more about Coach Micheal Burt. He's still a very active mentor in my life, and I work directly with him every week. Long story short, becoming a championship producer all starts with finding a mentor and finding a community.

I'm really proud of the community we've built. We've developed COACHG, which is home to hundreds of insurance agents—and soon, I believe, thousands—across the country. It's where we train, develop, and help agents reach that next level. And I think the most important thing COACHG provides is a community of people who've done it. No matter where you are—whether you're trying to write your first policy or hit $100K, $3 million, or $4 million—someone in that community has done it. And I believe it's incredibly important to have people who have already walked that journey to help guide you. So, find a mentor. Find a community.

The second thing? Find a proven, consistent system. This is one of the most important things. I talk about it all the time: whatever sales system you're using—as an individual agent or as a high-level producer—you need to start developing systems. You need to find systems that are teachable, duplicatable, and repeatable.

If you want to grow and build a championship team, this is the time—when you're still an individual producer, becoming a championship producer—to develop your systems. And how do you develop a system? You start by finding systems that have already worked. That, in my opinion, is the biggest life hack: you don't need to reinvent the wheel.

Find what's working. Find the *whos* that have the *hows*. Then, duplicate those proven models. You'll always make your own tweaks, but you need a system that's already been tested and proven. For us, one of our key systems is the "two-point plays"—our high-level sales strategy that allows you to package and sell multiple policies per client. We emphasize earning $1,200 in first-year commission per client during The Rookie Season. That's how we develop and onboard new agents. It's a very systematic process. When you join our company, you go through The Rookie Season, which is all about becoming a championship producer. What you need to do is either find a system like that or duplicate something similar—just make sure it's consistent and repeatable. Some people, as I said before, have no desire to build a team—and that's completely fine. But even if you just want to stay a championship producer, you still need a consistent, repeatable, and teachable system.

The next concept—one that has truly changed my life—is becoming an *Agent of Interest*. This is an idea I learned from Coach Micheal Burt. He teaches a very powerful concept called Person of Interest, which was also the title of his Wall Street bestselling book. I absolutely love the concept. It's all about how to get people to come to you—in droves. How do you attract high-quality customers? Partnerships? Opportunities? I took that idea and adapted it into what I call the Agent of Interest concept.

So, what does it mean to become an Agent of Interest? It means becoming the type of agent who attracts ideal consumers, ideal partnerships, and ideal people. When they see your face or your brand, they associate it with something specific—whatever you've built your brand around. I love teaching this concept, and it's a huge part of our process. We'll go deeper into it later in the book.

Now, tying back to the idea of systems—let's talk about having a *consistent process*. I always say that a consistent process equals consistent results. An inconsistent process equals inconsistent results. So when it comes to building a proven and consistent sales system, you also need to ask: what about your processes? Are they consistent? Are they repeatable? Are they teachable? Your processes, along with your systems, are critical—and you'll see that emphasized throughout this book.

Let's talk about consistent training. As a former coach, this is second nature to me. When I played football, we did the exact same drills every single day at the start of practice—stance and start, get-offs, rip moves, spin moves, all the fundamentals. Looking back, there was a reason for that. It became muscle memory. We did those things in games, because we had practiced them every single day. We trained on the same techniques, the same concepts—over and over. And it's no different in insurance or in business. You have to have consistent training. Travis Goveia, our national sales director, has a quote that I really love: "Training isn't something you did. It's something you do." It needs to be ongoing.

In our organization, we train every single day—and that's a real difference-maker. If you think you already know it all or believe you don't need to train like you used to, I guarantee that mindset is what's holding you back. You have to train consistently every single day. That's how you build muscle memory. That's how you sharpen the sword.

And I can't stress this enough: it's much better to be *sharply pointed* than *well-rounded*. Price Pritchett talks about this in *You2*—that breakthroughs come from focus, not from trying to be everything at once. We don't try to do one hundred different things at once. We focus on one thing and do it extremely well. For years I had rental properties, did some day or weekly trading, and always had a million side hustles. I made a decision one day after losing a good amount in the markets to get sharply focused on one business and the one I could truly control the outcome. So, in January 2022, I decided to focus solely on insurance and team building. The exponential growth since has proved that being sharply pointed (focused) beats well-rounded (diversified) any day of the week.

Know your numbers. I think one of the biggest areas I failed in early on was that I just went out and sold. I knocked on doors. I was Mr. Happy-Go-Lucky. But I didn't know much about business. I didn't have much business acumen. But numbers? Numbers tell you everything. You should be making decisions based on information. These days, all my decisions are data-driven.

Everything is backed by numbers. Knowing your numbers will help you make smarter, more valuable decisions. It'll help you make the *right* decisions. So track everything. And don't worry—we'll get into how to track things and what to measure as we move forward. These are the core components we're going to cover when it comes to becoming a championship producer. This is the foundation—the footers of your house. Without these, you're not going to be able to put up the walls. You're not going to be able to build the house. So this is where we're going to start this thing. I'm looking forward to taking you through it.

ONE
DRAFT THE RIGHT TEAM

Finding a mentor and community is something I've become extremely passionate about. The reason is simple: I speak to who I once was. I've been in the business for nine to ten years now. For the first five or six years, I was mostly doing it on my own. As I mentioned earlier, I worked with Michael Sams at Sams/Hockaday for about 15 months. But after that, for the next five years, it was really just me. I had a couple of agents, and we were out there grinding—just solo hoofing it along. And honestly, I thought I knew everything. Or maybe not everything—but I didn't know what I didn't know.

Over the last two to three years, I went all in on finding mentors and building a community. That decision has transformed both my life and our agency. As I reflect on the journey, I feel like I've narrowed down the key things you should look for when seeking out a mentor or a community. Just as importantly, you need to eliminate the bad apples and focus on the good ones. The first thing you'll hear me talk about throughout this book is

demonstrated capacity. What that means is this: have they actually *demonstrated* what they're teaching you?

For example, if someone comes to me wanting to build a $3–$5 million agency, I've demonstrated that I can do that at a high level. So in my opinion, I'm qualified to teach that. On the flip side, if I wanted to lose weight and get in shape, and the person offering to coach me was 300 pounds and clearly out of shape, that's not demonstrated capacity. I'd find someone who *is* in shape, someone with a proven process and system—someone who's done it at a high level. So when you're looking for a mentor, make sure they've actually done what you want to do—and done it well.

That leads me to my next point: find someone who has already achieved what you're trying to achieve. I always say it—*the "whos" will show you how*. People come to me all the time asking, "Chase, how do I do this? How do I do that?" And I always say: replace *how* with *who*. Dan Sullivan even wrote the book on it—*Who Not How*. The *who* will solve your problem—not the *how*. So ask yourself: *Who has done what I want to do?* Then go find them, pay them if you have to, and learn from them.

That mindset has completely changed my life. A few years ago, I found Justin Thomas Falck. He had a webinar system, and at the time, we were humming along—we had already crossed the million-dollar mark in our agency. But I felt stuck. We were knocking on doors, getting referrals, doing all the usual stuff, and I thought, *What's going to accelerate this?* I started researching systems that could generate leads—*inbound* leads. Leads from people who already knew us, liked us, and trusted us. A system that could work for me even while I was sleeping.

That's when I found Justin Thomas Falck. I paid him a good chunk of money—and that decision changed our business. We implemented his system—a proven lead generation strategy—and today, we bring in about 1,000 leads a week on average. That feeds our team, keeps them selling, and fills their calendars with automatically booked appointments. They don't have to do anything besides sell—and that's what allows us to attract a lot of high-level agents.

But if you strip that back a couple of years, when I was just a solo producer, that same setup was incredibly beneficial for our success. Instead of trying to figure out *how*, I figured out *who*—and that was a game-changer. I go back to Coach Burt. I wanted to develop a high-level coaching business. I had been a college coach. I'd been coaching for ten years. I missed that. I needed that. I *wanted* that. So I went to Coach Burt. He had proven to me that he had built a $10 million coaching business. And I thought, *You know what? I want a $10 million coaching business, too.* So I invested in a year of coaching with him. He taught me exactly how to do it. That's actually one of the reasons I'm writing this book today—Coach Burt even referred me to the publisher, which is such a cool, full-circle moment.

Long story short: I found the *who*. I didn't say, *How do I build a $10 million coaching business?* I said, *Who has done it?* And then I learned from them. That helped me fast-track my future. That *who* was Coach Burt. Since then, we've partnered on projects, spoken at events together, and done some really cool stuff. You never know—those *whos* you seek out may also be looking for *their* whos. There could be a partnership in the making. That mindset —focusing on the *who* rather than the *how*—has been truly life-changing. It's also important to find people you *resonate* with.

I always say that the people who come to us—who want to work with me or join our company—it's because they resonate with us. It's the same reason I gravitated toward Coach Burt or Justin Thomas Falck. These are people I really connected with. We share the same core values. We talk the same, think the same, act the same. Coach Burt was a coach—so when we talked, we spoke the same language. That made a big difference: working with someone I *resonated* with, someone who thought the way I did. Now that we've grown a team—and yes, this part is still rooted in being an individual producer—I think it's worth mentioning. Most of the people who come to work with us are former athletes, coaches, law enforcement professionals—people who thrive in structure. They're people who resonate with *me*. You attract who you are. That's why it's so important to seek out people and communities that align with you. A community that provides structure and accountability is crucial.

I mentioned COACHG earlier. I've been part of many different communities over the years. Sometimes they're seasonal—there for just a period in your life. And that's okay. It's natural to ebb and flow through different stages, and to find communities that fit where you are at the time. I've been in different Bible studies, clubs, and school groups—each one gave me what I needed in that particular moment. But I also believe in having a *consistent* community—one you can grow with year after year.

That's powerful. For me, that community has always been the insurance industry. I've made a lot of great friends here. We host events, we attend events—that's how we stay connected to the community and continue to grow together. Our biggest community within COACHG is The Coach's Office. It's a space we created that allows insurance agents from all over the country to connect, train, develop, lead, and see what's really working. Optimize, amplify, and then we scale—you'll hear me say that often. It's a community that challenges you, too.

And again, we go back to the *who's*—who is part of that community? Are there people you can mentor? People you can elevate? And, just as importantly, are there people who can elevate *you*? That, in my opinion, is one of the most essential things in life: continuing to be challenged, to get uncomfortable, and to grow. I often use this analogy from my football days: when we worked out, we literally lifted weights until our muscles tore. We tore them down so they could rebuild stronger. The right community does the same thing for your mind. It will challenge your thinking, break down your mental muscles, and help build them back up stronger—pushing you to the next level.

So, finding a community that encompasses all those things is key. I'm truly proud of The Coach's Office. It's a community that changes lives every day—and will continue to elevate others. I'm one of its biggest beneficiaries, because I get to host a group of people who also elevate *me*. I'm constantly seeking people—inside and outside my current circle—who can help take me to the next level. For example, Coach Burt has been someone who consistently pushes and elevates me. I also have other mentors in the insurance industry. Tony Holland, who sold over $100 million at one point in his career, challenges and pushes me like no other. Then there's John Hockaday and Jeff Sams—industry legends with 30 to 40 years of experience who have truly reached the mountaintop. Those are the kinds of people you need in your life: people you're helping, and people who are helping you. That exchange is what creates meaningful growth.

From personal experience, the biggest lesson I've learned is: **Don't do it alone.** You will never build anything great alone. As I mentioned earlier, the main difference-maker for me was realizing I couldn't figure everything out by myself. I thought I could. I thought I could learn it all alone. Remember that shift from "how" to "who"? If you're reading this book and you're in a place where you've been going it alone—maybe this is the first time you've gotten serious and you're ready for change—*find someone else*. Insurance can be a lonely business, especially if you're an independent agent or a solo producer. But it doesn't have to be. Find people who are doing it at a high level. It will change your life—and it will help you fast-track your success. That's one of my main goals for this book: to help you expedite your future. I spent three to five years knocking on doors and building a strong company, but I could have done it faster, easier, and with a lot fewer headaches if I had found the right mentors and community sooner. So please—*find someone*. Don't do it alone. Set yourself up to move faster and farther.

Let me come back to The Coach's Office. Within that program we also have what we call the Game Plan Community. What's really cool about this community is that it's designed specifically for agency owners and leadership. We've created a 24/7 space exclusively for agency leaders, where they can connect, share, and collaborate. We also host live calls for this community, where we dive into high-level topics like scaling, leadership, hiring and firing, systems, processes—you name it. These calls include hundreds of agents across the country. It's been a game-changing community. And it's allowed us to improve and evolve in ways that simply wouldn't be possible without it. We also have The Huddle community—that one's designed for *everyone*. It's built for agents, admin, leadership, and ownership. The focus is all around the sales process: generating revenue, improving our sales skills, and ultimately selling more products. It's a big call, and we host a couple of them regularly. We hold at least one Huddle every week, and honestly, I think it's one of the most important communities we offer.

It's also one of the most overlooked areas in most businesses. People tend to think, *Well, it's just selling*. But there's a big difference between *selling* and *selling at a high level*—and that's what we've really dialed in. In my opinion, we've developed the secret sauce for high-level sales. Our agents average a minimum of

$1,200 in first-year commission per client. That kind of performance allows us to grow at an exponential rate, while others might be lucky to earn a third of that. So, the Huddle community is definitely one of my favorites. It's a weekly call and community dedicated to driving your first-year revenue per client to new heights—and ultimately helping you develop a proven system.

TWO
RUN THE RIGHT ROUTE

Chapter Two is all about finding a consistent process—a proven system built on consistency and repeatability. As you'll learn throughout this book, my journey in the insurance industry started with a grind. During my first three years, I was taught to knock on doors. And let me tell you—it was just as miserable as it sounds. Knocking on doors *sucks*.

My daily goal was to knock on 25, maybe 30 doors. And if I was really lucky, I'd make one sale. When you have only one sale a day, you have to make the most of that opportunity. For me, that meant developing a sales system that allowed me to package and sell multiple policies in a single appointment. I had to uncover several different needs at once with that one client.

A lot of agents in the insurance industry just sell one policy. But very early in my career, I realized that wasn't going to work for me. I wasn't going to survive on single-policy sales. So I developed a system that allowed me to sell three, four, sometimes even five policies per client. That one client was essentially worth the value of multiple clients. Because if I had been selling only one policy per client, it could've taken five clients to produce what I was generating with just one. Without even knowing it at the time, I was already optimizing my sales process—consistently hitting that $1,200 first-year commission target per client very early on.

That was just normal to me. I didn't even realize that many agents were only selling one insurance product—just a Medicare plan, or just a life insurance policy, or just a cancer policy. Meanwhile, I was out there bundling all three, four, even five at once. I thought, *This is pretty cool. This is fun.* But more importantly, during that time, I was unknowingly developing my own proven, consistent, repeatable, and teachable sales process. That's what qualifies me today to teach and lead at a high level.

Coach Burt always says that when he thinks of me, he thinks of a *builder of teams*. I always say that's just a byproduct of my true skill—my real strength lies in teaching agents and agencies how to optimize their sales processes and systems. That's what enables you to build a team. So going back to the core idea here—it's critical that you find a *proven, consistent system* that you can develop, repeat, and eventually teach. And if you just want to remain a solo agent? That's awesome. This kind of system is exactly what makes a solo agent super successful. It also allows you to work less. But if you want to go to the next level, this is what will take you there: the ability to cross-sell effectively—and, in turn, teach others how to do it too.

When I talk about packaging and selling multiple policies to a single client, I'm really talking about cross-selling. I teach a monthly webinar and run a boot camp called The Cross-Sell King, where I dive deep into bundling and packaging strategies. We've developed a system we call The Umbrella System—a method for selling three, four, or even five policies at once. And it all hinges on one thing: effective cross-selling. So how do we do that? We uncover those opportunities through our sales process.

Our client needs assessment—I'll get into that in just a second. But the repeatable portion of this is the most important. When I teach, talk to, and educate agents and agencies, it's all about repetition. We always go back to that analogy of sports. Most of you have probably played a sport at some point in your life. When you warm up for a sport—whether it's basketball and you're doing layups, football and you're tossing the ball around, or golf and you're starting at the driving range—you're getting ready. You're preparing. And that's exactly what we do when it comes to selling insurance. We have the warm-up—the repeatable process. And that process is the client needs assessment. I'll focus on that here in the book because it's our repeatable, proven method. It's what drives a lot of those ancillary sales. It helps us uncover opportunities, start conversations, and pull out needs like retirement planning, annuities, and more. It's highly repeatable—and more importantly, it's teachable.

I teach this process to agents and agencies all over the country, whether through public or private boot camps. It's like singing the same song over and over again—like that Journey song, "Don't Stop Believin'." You know they might be tired of singing it, but it's the moneymaker. And that's what the client needs assessment is. I've taught it thousands of times. I never deviate. I teach it the same way because it's the smash hit that everyone wants to hear—and it works. And honestly, it's what drives more revenue into your agency: having a repeatable, teachable, systematic, and scalable system.

That word—**systematic**—is super important. We start with the client needs assessment. We use a flowchart to make sure we're walking through the appointment the right way. We teach a very systematic method for transitioning through the appointment and a very systematic approach to delivering the sale. It's got to be systematic, teachable, and scalable.

Can I teach this to the masses? Can I deliver it to the masses? When I'm speaking to consumers—people buying insurance policies—I need to be able to teach, explain, and communicate this clearly to large groups. We run weekly webinars with 1,000 to 1,500 attendees. So the question becomes: Will it make sense to that many people, from all walks of life, all at once? That's where scalability comes in.

So finding a proven, consistent system or process—these are the keys to building an incredible foundation. This is the kind of stuff we focus on in The Coach's Office. That's our two-point playbook. It's where I teach our exact sales system. "The Rookie Season"—that's what we call our structured training for new agents. It's not just about having a sales system; it's about having a system for onboarding new agents.

Is it repeatable? Scalable? Duplicatable? We've locked that down, too, and we've put it all into video format. And that's what you should be thinking about right now, even as a solo agent. Start developing. Start filming. Start documenting. Start putting your processes and systems into a format that's duplicatable and repeatable—and you'll have your foundation for success.

If there's one takeaway from this chapter, it's this: you don't have to do this alone—and you shouldn't. The right mentor can accelerate your growth, and the right community can multiply it. Surround yourself with people who challenge you, believe in you, and have already walked the path you want to walk. That's where momentum is built. That's where transformation happens. Whether it's through The Coach's Office, The Game Plan, The Huddle, or a completely different circle—find your people, plug in, and commit. Your future moves faster when you're not carrying it alone.

THREE
AGENT OF INTEREST

Let's talk about becoming an Agent of Interest. Teaching this concept has quickly become one of my newfound passions. I just finished teaching our live boot camp with Coach Micheal Burt. We took his *Person of Interest* strategy—made popular through his book and teachings—switched out some of the wording, added our own teaching points, and developed the idea of the Agent of Interest. So—how do you become an Agent of Interest who attracts ideal consumers, ideal agents, ideal partnerships, and ideal opportunities into your life and business?

What I was missing for years was a true brand. But I believe we've finally built one. For our consumer-facing company, Gruening Health and Wealth, we've created a solid brand. And personally, we've built "COACHG" as a brand for our coaching and training company. I genuinely believe there's a formula to it. Once you figure out that formula, it's life-changing. Right now, it's honestly overwhelming. Every day, my phone is blowing up. Just last night, after teaching the Coach's Headset Boot Camp, I picked up my phone—twenty missed text messages, twenty missed calls, and fifty emails. Agents are reaching out. Consumers are calling. Partnerships are forming. It's an incredible place to be.

But it took a lot of intention. It didn't happen overnight. It was very deliberate. The hardest part is breaking through. It reminds me of the concept "Sheehan's Wall," a theory developed by Peter Sheehan. Imagine a big brick wall, and you're holding a sledgehammer. Now, if you swing that hammer at random spots all over the wall, it'll take forever to bring it down. But if you strike the same spot, over and over—ten, fifteen, twenty times—that wall breaks down much faster. That's the approach I urge you to take when building your brand, attracting your ideal client, and owning your sales process: consistent, focused effort. That's Sheehan's Wall. Becoming a person—or agent—of interest isn't as complicated as it seems. It's really about putting yourself out there.

I'll walk through a few ways you can start doing that:

- Social media
- YouTube
- Podcasting
- Writing books
- Websites
- Emails
- Newsletters
- Credentials
- Even your voicemail signature.

All these things contribute to the main goal.

If you've got a piece of paper nearby, draw a circle in the middle and write "Agent of Interest" in it. Then, think about how many different connection points you can create to feed that central goal. That's exactly what we did while building Gruening

Health and Wealth, our Medicare and retirement shop, over the past 10 years. We posted on social media *every single day*. Educational clips. Photos of our agents with senior clients. Helpful tips. Every day. And I remember a few years ago, someone said to me, "Man, you're really good—you guys are big-time. I see you on social media every day." And honestly, we weren't anything huge at the time. But perception is reality. Social media is a *free billboard*. It's crazy. It doesn't cost you anything, and you can get in front of people daily. So whatever your ideal message is—whatever your ideal client looks like—put that message out there every single day.

And here's a little bonus tip: For years, since we specialize in Medicare and retirement, if someone looked even close to 65, I'd add them as a friend on Facebook. I did this for years—just adding people who looked around 65. And because I was posting about Medicare and retirement planning every single day, people would randomly reach out. They'd say, "Hey, for some reason, we're Facebook friends, and I see you do Medicare and retirement planning. I'm turning 65 and could use some help." And I'd think, *I know exactly how you found me—I added you at some point.* Now, I use the exact same strategy with insurance agents. So, whoever your ideal client is—add them on Facebook and post relevant content consistently.

I also took it a step further. These days, anyone who follows me on social media sees educational content for agents *every single day*. I've applied the same strategy for both sides of the business: once to become an Agent of Interest in the consumer space, and now to attract agents. The only difference is the content. Same frequency—different focus.

And *that* frequency and consistency is the secret sauce when it comes to social media. You have to be consistent. You have to show up often. We actually hired a company that now posts twice a day across five platforms and manages both long- and short-form YouTube content. It's been a total game-changer.

Write this down: **When you take yourself seriously, other people take you seriously.** It won't happen until you take yourself seriously—I promise you that. Nobody will take your insurance agency seriously unless *you* do. That's where the game shifts.

Let's talk about YouTube. Man, I never touched YouTube before. But about a year ago, after hiring our content team, they told me, "You *have* to be on YouTube." Now they film and edit short-form clips and upload them regularly. Even before we hired them, I'd started filming and uploading content myself. And here's what's awesome about YouTube: unlike Instagram or Facebook—where your content lives and dies in just a couple of days—YouTube actually builds momentum over time. You put good content out there, and people can find it *years later*. I know multiple huge agencies across the country that don't spend a dime on marketing. It's all organic content from YouTube—they built their entire presence that way. So you could be developing your agent brand—or your personal brand—on YouTube right now.

Podcasting has also become a huge passion of mine. Looking back, if I could do it again, I *definitely* would have launched a podcast on the consumer side—for Medicare and insurance. I didn't then, but now we're doing it for the COACHG brand—and I absolutely love it. I've had the chance to interview some of the top names out there:

- Terry Blachek, co-founder of Orangetheory, which sold for tens of millions
- Tony Holland, who exited the insurance industry with a nine-figure deal

- Chuck McDowell, who runs a $100 million-a-year mortgage company and is the nation's leading expert in timeshare exits
- Coach Burt, Matt Temmen, Joe Pate, and many others

And I can't wait to see who's next. It's been an incredible way to share my message and attract business leaders from all over the country. If you watch any episode on our YouTube channel, you'll hear me talk about The Coach's Office and our brand—every time. You're going to see me talk about how to go deeper with us. It's just another touchpoint—another way for your clients to find you, learn about you, and engage with you.

I always emphasize what I call the *assumption gap*. Everything I'm talking about here helps you fill that gap. When someone sees you for the first time, all they have to go on is their first impression—and whatever assumptions they make about you. The second time they interact with you, they start forming more of an opinion. That opinion might be good or bad, but here's the key: you can actually influence what they assume or believe about you through the frequency and quality of your touchpoints. If someone sees my content every day—my podcast, YouTube videos, social media posts, emails, newsletters, website—I'm filling those assumption gaps with the narrative *I* want to give them. And that's exactly what you're doing when you become an Agent of Interest. You're shaping the story people tell themselves about who you are. You're taking control of how people perceive you and your brand. That's what's so powerful about becoming an agent, person, or agency of interest.

Books are another way of doing this. I'm currently writing two books: one for Medicare consumers, and one for insurance agents. And while I'm having a lot of fun with them, make no mistake—they're also lead magnets. They're another chance for people to learn about me, go deeper with me, and fill that assumption gap with meaningful content.

If you're not putting out a professional website with strong content, solid creative, and good search engine optimization, you're missing the boat. Your website needs to rank well, look sharp, and function smoothly.

Don't be sloppy with emails. Have a clean, professional signature. Include your picture. Make sure people know how to contact you. Make it look like you know what you're doing and that you're someone worth working with. If your email just ends with *"Chase Gruening"* and nothing else, that's not professional, and it's definitely not high-level. Tighten up your email signature.

We've got newsletters on autopilot for everything we do. We send out a weekly newsletter titled "Halftime" for agents and educational newsletters for consumers, and this has been a huge game-changer.

With credentials, on the Medicare and retirement side, something as simple as paying the fee to become BBB-accredited made a big difference. When people show resistance, we just direct them to that BBB profile. We talk to clients in all 50 states, and we need that level of credibility. Google my business—we've got over 500 five-star reviews. That's a big deal. It matters.

And finally, voicemails—this one's a pet peeve of mine. It drives me nuts when I call an agent and get a robotic message. I want to know I've reached a *real* professional, someone I can actually connect with. So here's what I always recommend: if you respond to texts, say that in your voicemail. Something like: "Hey, this is Chase. Sorry I missed your call—I'd love to connect. If it's easier, shoot me a quick text, and I'll get back to you as soon as I can. Or feel free to leave a message, and I'll talk to you soon." Little things like that can make a big difference in how people perceive you. It's pretty simple—but I don't want to hear, "You have reached

217-*blah-blah-blah*. Please leave a message." So tighten up those voicemails and keep them professional.

The result of all this? It opens doors you never thought were possible. Partnerships happen. People take you seriously *when you take yourself seriously*. As a result of this consistent branding and messaging, we've developed incredible partnerships on the consumer side. One local hospital sends us Medicare beneficiaries—and we don't pay a dime for those referrals. We also run the Medicare division for a large property and casualty shop. And we've built smaller partnerships across the country. That's just the consumer side.

On the agent side, we have agents reaching out to us daily—and I'm incredibly thankful for that. But it's the result of consistent, frequent action that delivers value and communicates our message at a high level. Once you become an Agent of Interest, a Person of Interest, or even an *agency* of interest—life changes. I encourage you to get comfortable being uncomfortable. Put your message out there. You'll attract the people who align with who you are and what you offer. And just as importantly, you'll repel the ones who don't resonate with your message. That's a good thing. So use every available touchpoint—put yourself out there—and watch everything grow from there.

FOUR
FILL THE STANDS

Lead generation is arguably one of the most important topics. You can be the best agent or the best agency in the country, but if you don't have people to talk to—if there's no one to sell your product to—then it doesn't matter. You need leads.

Let's do a quick exercise: grab a piece of paper and draw a circle. In the middle, write *"Lead Generation."* Now, think about how many different lead sources you can connect to that circle. Here's what's in mine:

- Events
- Seminars
- Webinars
- Mailers
- Paid advertising
- Strategic partnerships
- Billboards
- Commercials
- Books

- Podcasts
- Social media

Every one of these ties into lead generation. It's important we dig into each of these, so let's start by sticking to the insurance agency context for this next section.

Write this note down: "The road to the many is through the one." What does that mean? How many people can you deliver your message to in one setting? I prefer formats where I can teach many people at once. I don't do one-on-one teaching. I don't do one-on-one coaching. I like to teach to groups—and events are a great way to do that.

We participate in senior events and other large community events where we set up a booth and have the opportunity to interact with hundreds, sometimes thousands, of people. Events are cost-effective—usually only $100 to $300 to set up a booth—and they give you the chance to share your message with a broad audience. We usually offer a giveaway (like a gift box or TV) to collect information and position ourselves as a valuable local resource. It's a great way to implement your "Agent of Interest" strategy.

Seminars are another big one. Educational seminars are popular in the industry—and they work. I do have a few recommendations, though: First, whenever possible, do them for free. I also strongly recommend not hosting "food seminars." I know some people will disagree with me on that, but I don't like spending money on meals and beverages for attendees. There are better ways to attract people who are genuinely interested. We want people to attend our seminars for the *education*—not just for the food. We call those folks "plate lickers." That's why we emphasize delivering real value and meaningful education.

To avoid attracting the wrong audience, we hold our seminars in-house. We have a couple of brick-and-mortar offices, and that's where we host them. If you have an office, I highly recommend doing the same. In-house seminars are incredibly efficient. You don't have to leave the building, and there's almost no prep time. You gain so much time back in your day. Libraries and community centers are also great locations for hosting seminars if you don't have your own space. I'll go into how we promote those seminars in a moment.

Webinars are our favorite. We bring in a thousand people every week through webinars and paid advertising. That's our primary lead generation source. Everything else just fills the gaps.

Mailers: when I was just starting out in the industry, I worked out of my mom's basement. I remember stuffing envelopes by hand and mailing them out to people within a forty-five-mile radius. It *still* works. Some people continue to use this method. I don't think it delivers the highest return on investment—but it's definitely still effective. A few weeks ago, I sat down with my buddy Matt Temmen. He actually *mails books*. He's got a Medicare book that he sends out across the country—and I love this method. He's got it down to a science and even owns a print shop, so his setup is unique. But here's the takeaway: *no one throws away a book*. If I were doing direct mail today, I'd focus on including something people won't throw away. Back in the day, I used to include magnets—people love magnets, especially older folks, who put them on the fridge. So ask yourself: *"What can I include in that mailer that someone will keep?"* That's where the magic is.

Online Ads / Paid Advertising is one of my favorites, but it depends. I worked with Justin Thomas Falck to develop our system. And here's the truth: paid ads can get *very* expensive. I don't recommend jumping into paid ads unless your sales process is fully optimized. **Remember: optimize before you amplify.** If you're optimized, you might be ready for ads. But your lead cost can vary—$5, $10, $15 or more per lead—and it all depends on how good your ads are and what kind of return you're seeing. Paid ads can be your best friend or your worst enemy. It all depends on how good your system is and how well you're generating and converting leads.

Strategic Partnerships: If I could go back, I'd focus even more on this. Can you develop partnerships with organizations that already serve your ideal client? For us, it's been hospitals, property and casualty agencies, financial advisors—people who already work with retirees. We step in, offer a holistic solution, and offload Medicare-related education and services. It costs them nothing, and we provide real value. It's a win-win. So ask yourself: *"Who can I help in this way? Who can I partner with to take care of the questions and problems they're facing?"*

Billboards and commercials are really interesting. We do a lot of billboards now—but I *don't* recommend billboards or commercials if you're a solo shop. This is more of a down-the-road strategy. Billboards and commercials are great, but they're best suited for when you're operating at scale. What I've found is that they're especially effective for attracting partnerships. Again, when you take yourself seriously, *others*—especially potential partners—start to take you seriously, too. People want to work with the biggest show in town. Now, if you're solo, you *could* do one or two billboards—but I don't think you'll see much return unless you go all in. One or two won't move the needle. In one of our local markets, we've got 15 billboards running, and it's that *frequency* that makes the impact.

So, as I wrap up this section, here's the big takeaway: whatever you choose to focus on, think about how you can teach and educate *many* people at once. It's simple math—if you're doing one-to-one teaching, you just won't generate as much lead flow.

We need to focus on ways to generate leads in bulk, in one sitting—through events, seminars, webinars, and online advertising. When I was door-knocking, I wasn't reaching many people at once. Sure, it worked for me back then—mainly because it was free and I had no overhead in my early 20s. But that's why I don't even include door-knocking on the list today. You can technically add it, but I don't recommend it.

The biggest takeaway here is this: if you've still got that circle on your paper with "Lead Generation" in the middle, and all the different touchpoints around it—the key ingredient to make it all work is *frequency*. Some people will only take action after encountering a combination of those touchpoints. For example:

- Someone might see us on social media, then meet us at an event—and that's what gets them to act.
- Someone else might attend a seminar and receive a mailer—that combo moves them forward.
- Another might see a billboard, hear a radio ad, and then catch a commercial—and after that third exposure, *now* they're ready to take action.

So frequency is key.

And finally, if you're a new agent—a solo producer—start by focusing on just one or two strategies. Pick your lanes and go all in. Like I always say, pound them into the ground like you're swinging a sledgehammer at Sheehan's Wall.

FIVE
REPS WIN GAMES

This chapter is all about consistent training. Most producers lack consistent training and a focus on optimizing internally before looking externally. I see so many agents and agencies obsessed with marketing. It's marketing, marketing, marketing. And listen, I love marketing. We spend millions of dollars a year on it. But not *before* we optimized and looked inward. Too many people want to skip steps.

They throw a bunch of money at things without first optimizing, and they stay stuck. You're constantly dumping money into systems that don't work. I can't say this enough:

Optimize first. Then amplify.

Here's the deal: if I'm generating $1,200 in first-year commission per client, and you're generating $300 or $600, then all you're doing is amplifying a weaker sales process. We don't do that. We've built a highly optimized operation—and *then* we pour marketing dollars on top of it to amplify something that already works. That's what this chapter is about: **how do you build an optimized internal system and sales process?**

First step: Weekly meetings.

If you're a solo producer, your weekly meeting might be with your mentor, your community, or whoever you're plugged in with. If you're in The Coach's Office, that's your Huddle, Game Plan, and Practice Field sessions. We've built those in for you. If you've got a team—even a small one—hold consistent weekly meetings. For us, we meet every Monday at 8:00 AM. That's one of my biggest non-negotiables. Everyone is up and ready. We set the tone for the week.

These meetings are about more than just logistics—they're about *communication*. Often, it's not what you say, but *how* you deliver it that matters. So ask yourself: *"How am I communicating?"* Are you giving your team a clear, weekly game plan? We even have our agents write out a daily game plan—so we know exactly what their day looks like. Don't get complacent. You have to keep learning.

I remember when I was a solo agent. I'd finally moved out of my mom's basement—believe it or not—and within a year, I was making six figures, nearly $200,000 at 26 years old. There were days I'd just hit the gym or ride my bike on the trails. It was a nice day outside. I had the freedom. But looking back, I was getting complacent. And complacency is a killer.

Not having a mentor or a strong community in those early years set me back. I got too comfortable. And that's dangerous. You have to keep learning. You have to get uncomfortable. You have to see what's out there.

Boot camps are one of the biggest ways we train and develop. We run several popular ones. Just yesterday, I ran the Coach's Headset. I put on a gamer-style headset and did live calls with real prospects—consumers we'd never spoken to before. I walked the walk. I followed our sales process live, in real time. I did it for our internal team and our Coach's Office members. We had 65 agents on that call—and every single one of them was blown away. Now, for me, that's muscle memory. I've been doing this process for 10 years. But for many agents on that call, it wasn't. That was their training. That was their mentorship. And guess what? Just since yesterday, several agents from that session have already written new business.

We also have the Agent of Interest Boot Camp, which teaches you, in-depth, how to build your brand and attract ideal clients and partnerships. Then there's The Cross-Sell King—one of my personal favorites. It's all about cross-selling and packaging. I teach products, the full sales system, and how to effectively integrate both. The Rookie Season is built for new agents. It covers onboarding, training, and early development. And then there's Chalk Talk, where I bring in industry leaders—people generating multiple millions in revenue—and we dive into scaling, strategy, and high-level systems. Within our organization, we have boot camps for every stage of your journey.

But here's the thing: I don't care if you train with us or with someone else. What matters is that you have consistent training, consistent systems, and something you're plugging into regularly. This changed the game for me. It's that old saying: if you hang around three or four unmotivated, negative people, you'll be the fourth. But the opposite is also true—if you surround yourself with three or four people more successful than you, you'll become the fifth. Consistent training put me around high performers. And I thought to myself, *I don't want them writing more business than me. I want to be at their level—or higher.* That mindset shifted everything.

We also have a 24/7 message board and community app for our members and partners. While writing this book, I checked my phone and saw a few agents asking questions in there. It's a space where people communicate, support each other, and get answers around the clock. Do *you* have that kind of community? Somewhere you can consistently connect, learn, and grow? You need consistent ways to train and develop—whether that's through events, seminars, or professional development opportunities.

I used to be a big skeptic when it came to events and seminars. I didn't believe in them. But I've changed my stance—with a caveat. You have to be an educated buyer. There's a lot of fluff out there. A lot of phonies. Look for events that deliver real value. Events where you walk away with actionable insights—not just sales pitches. And if there *is* a sale at the end, make sure what they're offering is of extreme value, and that it's backed by proven results.

For us, we run our Annual Playbook event, where we cover cross-selling, packaging, AI, advertising, and more. Then we've got our more laid-back event, the Coach's Retreat at the Beach, which happens in Destin every April. I'm super excited about this one—it's my favorite. We've got a few more sprinkled throughout the year, but those are two of the big ones.

There are tons of industry events you can attend. Just make sure you're educated. Choose the ones that align with where you're at in your career—and where you're trying to go. You need to invest in professional development. You need to be around other people—people doing bigger things, and yes, even people doing *smaller* things than you. That's important, too. Surround yourself with both. Learn from all directions. Keep showing up. One of the reasons I do what I do is because I love providing value to the person I once was. I truly believe it's our responsibility to give back—to provide value to others. We have to be people who give value more than anything. There are people in our lives that we give value to—and people we receive value from. It's part of the circle of life, and it's important that we keep that cycle going.

Webinars: I'm always doing free webinars for the public.

Some of my favorites include The Cross-Sell King, Branding on a Budget (taught by my wife, Emily—she'll be sharing more on that later in this book), and Building Championship Producers and Teams. Each of these webinars has a different focus and different takeaways, but they're all easy, accessible ways to engage, learn, and train. There are also a lot of industry webinars out there that are topic-specific and could be incredibly relevant to where you are in your career or life. Just make sure you're seeking out what's *relevant to you*—and showing up for it. That's the key.

Couples Retreat: This is something I'm really excited about. Emily and I have been tossing around the idea of hosting a couples retreat specifically for insurance agents, and I think we're getting close to launching it. Years ago, we attended a couples retreat designed for business owners. It focused on how to live with a super-driven spouse and build both a successful business and a strong marriage. And I don't want to lose sight of that message: we need training in *every* aspect of our lives. It's not just about insurance. It's about business, relationships, and personal growth. For us, the retreat we attended covered a little of all three—and it didn't hurt that it was on the beach. We wanted to grow as a couple, not just in business, but in our marriage as well.

So, I want to close this chapter with this thought: in any area of your life—whether it's insurance, business, marriage, or something else—you've got to find ways to train and grow. There are so many resources out there. Use them. Don't do it alone. Be consistent. That's what really moves the needle. Training isn't something we *did*. It's something we *do*.

SIX
WATCH THE FILM

This chapter is all about knowing your numbers—and in full transparency, I feel like I'm still seeking guidance in this area. Now, don't get me wrong—I *know* our numbers, and we have exceptional ones. But if we all have our kryptonite or area of weakness, this is mine. It's the area I'd like to be stronger in. I think many of us are harder on ourselves, but honestly, this is one of the most important areas: knowing your numbers.

One thing I always say is: *information is power*. Information allows us to make better decisions—*data-driven* decisions—and helps us remove emotion from the equation. In the early stages of my career, I made a lot of emotional or non-data-backed decisions. With the right data, those decisions could have been a lot better.

In this chapter, I'm going to walk through some key numbers you need to know early on as a solo producer or agency owner. These numbers will help you grow, make better decisions, and run a stronger operation.

Revenue

First off, we base everything on revenue—because revenue is what fuels your business. Without it, you can't function. You can't cover overhead, invest in systems or people, or grow. That's why it's critical to make revenue a central focus in your metrics and tracking. I remember, early on, we used to track apps and premium per product as our main metrics. But I quickly realized that apps and product premiums don't pay the bills—revenue does. So we adjusted accordingly.

Next up—if you've seen me on social media or heard me speak, you've probably heard me say this:

First-Year Commission per Client (FYC)

This is my favorite metric to talk about. FYC is simply how much commission you generate from a new client in their first year. In our industry—Medicare and retirement—many agents only sell a Medicare policy, which typically brings in $300 to $600 in first-year commission. The difference with us and the producers we work with in The Coach's Office, is that we aim to get you to $1,200 in first-year commission per client. I believe that once you hit that number, you're running an optimized business. How do you get there? Through effective cross-selling, packaging, and offering multiple solutions. It's easy to calculate. For every new client, ask: *How much first-year commission did I generate?* If it's not $1,200, there's room to optimize. That's your benchmark.

Cash Flow

This one's straightforward—but critical. When I say cash flow, I mean *net cash flow*: how much money is left after your expenses are paid. That's your income minus expenses—your net, your bottom line. This is something you need to know. As a solo agency, tools like QuickBooks can be your best friend. Connect your bank accounts, credit cards, and business accounts. Tag your expenses properly, track your income, and you'll have a clear view of your monthly, quarterly, and annual cash flow. You *must* know your net. You *must* know your bottom line.

Return On Ad Spend (ROAS)

How much are you spending on ads, and how much are you getting back? First-year commission minus ad spend—that's your ROAS. If you had to focus on just one metric, first-year commission ROAS is the one. Everything else is just numbers and calculations. We monitor monthly production per agent, per product, and per application. We like looking at things on a monthly basis. One thing I was always told in the insurance industry: you can have a bad day, you can have a bad week, but you should never have a bad month. That's why I love monthly tracking—it tells the full story.

Lifetime Value

You want to be conservative with this. In the insurance business, there are a lot of residuals. Let's say a client generates a guaranteed $300 annual residual or renewal. Typically, we use a 2–3 year lifetime value, even though the actual value is often higher. To stay conservative, we take the annual residual and multiply it by three. That gives us the client's lifetime value. This is especially important if you're considering acquisitions, because that's what others will look at too.

When I speak, the two things I talk about most are: how much commission are you generating per product (revenue), and what's your average first-year commission per client? We love analyzing our revenue by product, and you might be surprised—our entry point, Medicare, is not our highest-commission product. It's actually retirement planning and supplementary health products. So our entry point is just that—an entry point. It allows us to have product diversification, portfolio diversification, and, ultimately, a diverse commission across product lines. Then there's annual production—we want to see the big picture, and that's what I love looking at. Right now, I'm reviewing last year's production and making projections based on what we're doing in the first quarter. It's usually pretty accurate and tells a clear story—showing our growth and how this year compares to last year. I love tracking those numbers.

Lead source is another key area. It's not a number, per se, but it's incredibly important to know where your leads are coming from. We use online advertising, billboards, commercials, radio, word of mouth, and strategic partnerships. Knowing the lead source helps us decide where to allocate marketing spend.

Then there's a data point we track called cost per registration. Since we do a lot of online advertising, we want to know which ads have the lowest cost per registration and what they're actually generating. That's critical. For Facebook and Instagram, we typically aim for a $5 cost per registration or lower.

A new metric we've started tracking is the annuity-to-new-client ratio. In our agency, we currently generate one annuity for every twenty-one new clients, which is a fantastic number. Tracking this helps us make projections and shows just how valuable our Medicare pipeline is—it brings in a whole new revenue stream without adding any overhead.

This chapter dives into the weeds a bit with numbers, but these are the things you absolutely need to know. In The Coach's

Office, we provide templates, tracking tools, organized documents, and systems to keep everything in order. These are must-haves. I went years without tracking this stuff, and if I'd had the right information earlier, I could have made much better decisions. So knowing your numbers is going to make a major difference in your ability to grow and scale efficiently.

SEVEN
ME TO WE

We're getting closer to wrapping up the first section of this book about becoming a truly successful championship producer. And you know what? It's perfectly okay if your goal is simply to be a championship producer—to run a solo shop. I never thought I'd build a massive agency or a big team. For four to five years, my focus was solely on becoming the best producer I could be.

I wanted to compete. I wanted to win the awards. I wanted to be the absolute best at what I did. And if that's your mission—to be a solo producer—then that's exactly where your focus should be: maximizing your personal production, being as efficient and profitable as possible, and optimizing your internal systems. First-year commissions, operational efficiency, and internal optimization are key. If you get those right, you'll always have the freedom to either remain a solo producer or eventually build a team. But in my opinion, you can't successfully build a team without first being a strong solo producer and agency owner. So, this chapter is really about the things I wish I'd done differently.

The way I see it, this book is about expediting your future

through my past. And I fully believe in that idea: you're most uniquely qualified to teach the person you once were. I was once a solo agent. I wouldn't say I was struggling, but it definitely could have been better. That's what this chapter is about—looking back and asking: how could I have gotten out of my mom's basement faster? How could I have expedited my growth? Hopefully, this helps you learn from some of my—let's call them shortcomings, not failures.

The first thing I wish I'd done sooner—network. I wish I had found a community, a group of like-minded individuals, a team, or a platform to be a part of. That's exactly why I built The Coach's Office—for the version of me who needed it back then, to help others fast-track their progress. I think of Brandon De La Peña. Love the guy. He's 23 years old and jumped into the insurance industry without a clue what he was doing. I wouldn't have either at 23. But he joined The Coach's Office, joined our downline, and was producing $20K a month within nine months of starting—all because he found a community and surrounded himself with people on the same path. That kind of support changed everything for him. I wasn't anywhere close to that at his age. So find a community. Or find a mentor. Either way, don't do it alone.

The second thing is cross-sell from day one. I see it all the time—new agents, solo agents, inexperienced agents—they miss this. And it's not rocket science: if you sell more policies per client, you'll scale faster. When we bring on new agents now, it's amazing—many of them only know how to sell three, four, or even five policies per client from the start. I think of Nic Stevens and Devin Curtis, part of our internal team—the very first sales they ever made were what we call "umbrella twos and threes." They sold multiple policies right out of the gate. That might sound mindblowing to some agents, but for them, that was just normal. It's all they ever knew. And if that's your baseline from day one, it's going to change the game for you. If you're not cross-selling right now—if you're not packaging at a high level—that can be a game-changer. I've even been dubbed the "Cross-Sell King" before. That's really what I'm best known for: teaching people how to package and increase their first-year commission, which unlocks everything else in your business. That's the biggest thing. If you don't know how to do that, we have the Two-Point Plays. It's a simple, systematic approach to cross-selling and packaging. I've been teaching it for years, and it's tried and true. I love it, baby.

Third point: hire sooner. I can't emphasize this enough—when you hire correctly, that person should actually make you money. The biggest misconception is, "Oh my God, it's going to cost me so much, I can't afford it." Well, then you're not hiring right. Because a good hire is an investment in your business. If you hire an admin for $50,000 a year, that should free up enough time for you to make $100,000 a year. Who wouldn't trade $50,000 for $100,000? Who wouldn't put $1 in an ATM and get $2 back? Just about everybody would. When you look at it that way, hiring becomes a no-brainer.

Looking back, I would've hired sooner. A lot of people wait and wait, thinking they're not ready. But I'll tell you—when you hire someone, when you lease an office, when you make a big move—it forces you to rise to the occasion. It pushes you to grow, to get better, and to make the investment worth it.

Also, hire your weakness. That's one thing my wife Emily (you'll hear more about her later in the book) always talks about—focus on your strengths and hire your weaknesses. That's been huge for me. I'm not naturally organized. I'm not good at making documents look pretty. But our admin team? Phenomenal at that. And now that I know my weaknesses, I don't even try to handle those things anymore. I also know that I can be a little too direct at times, and sometimes, it's better for others to step in and communicate things on my behalf. That level of self-awareness is key. When it comes to hiring agents, a lot of people wait too long. For me, I hired agents on a commission-only basis. I didn't have a lot of overhead. Or at least, I didn't think I did. There are a lot of ways to hire agents without taking on major costs.

And here's something we don't talk about enough: fire sooner. It's okay to part ways with people. That's a big life lesson I'm still learning—different people are meant for different seasons in your life. One thing I always ask from our team now is simple: just grow. I don't care if it's 100% growth year-over-year or just small steps forward—just don't go backward. That growth doesn't have to be a huge number. It just has to be intentional. There should be *some* kind of measurable progress—even if it's 5%, 10%, 15%—that shows we're moving forward. So, be ready to hire. Be ready to fire. Hire your weaknesses. Focus on your strengths.

Record everything. I can't say this enough. Social media has completely changed the game for us, and I went *years* without recording anything I was doing. I mean, if you're a solo agent—a championship producer—you're clearly doing something really, really well. You need to document those methods so you can duplicate them, repeat them, train others, and build on that success. Especially your processes. So if you're a solo producer looking to start a team or bring on an admin, record everything you're doing process-wise. That way, when you hire that administrative assistant, you can hand them a set of videos: *This is how we do it.* You've already recorded it. It becomes your SOP—your standard operating procedure—in video format.

Finally, reinvest more early on. I can't emphasize this enough. It's your business, and you have to spend money to make money. Think about Amazon and Tesla—do you think they hesitate to spend money? Of course not. It's just numbers. The difference is you're working with smaller numbers in the beginning. In my first few years, my profit margin was incredibly high. I hardly spent anything. It was all organic and grassroots—probably a 10% expense ratio and 90% profit margin.

But today, we operate closer to a 20%–30% expense ratio because of how aggressively we're reinvesting back into the business. And like I said earlier, when you take yourself seriously, other people take you seriously. You've got to reinvest in your business—whether that's in technology, people, office space, modernizing your systems, branding, marketing, joining a community, or finding a mentor. Reinvest. Every investment should make you more money. And if it doesn't, it's not a good investment. Ask yourself: *"Will this make me more money, or save me time (money)?"* If the answer is no, then it's probably not the right place to put your money.

Now, about developing your strengths, I've come to believe it's better to be sharply pointed than well-rounded (as I mentioned earlier). I used to think I needed to do everything, wear all the hats. But instead, be the sledgehammer to the brick wall—focused, consistent, and relentless in one spot. Double down on your strengths. Elevate them. Focus on them. Surround yourself with people who can offset your weaknesses. That will change the game. And if you're reading this book, doing it all on your own, you need to be part of The Coach's Office—a community that will expedite your growth, elevate your performance, and give you a touchpoint for everything you need to build your business. I've loved this first section of the book. Now, as we transition, we're moving on to the next level—*building a championship team.*

SECTION 1: CONCLUSION

As we wrap up Section 1 on becoming a championship producer, I have a note in my journal labeled "The Aha Moment"—and that's exactly what it was. I remember sitting there, pounding my head against the wall, thinking, *I can only do so much on my own.*

I could write six or seven hundred applications a year, but I couldn't go much further. There just wasn't enough time in the day. Then it hit me—what if I could teach two, three, even four people to do *half* of what I do? That would still be 200% of what I could accomplish alone. That was the big aha moment. It stopped being about me. The question became: *Can I teach others to be half as good as I am? Or three-fourths as good?* We all think we're the best producer in the world—I get it.

Most people reading this probably feel that way too. But at the end of the day, that doesn't matter. You can only do so much. There's only so much *you* can physically produce. That realization was huge for me. If I could teach others to do what I do—well, that's when things could really grow into a team. I started bringing on Travis and Jack early in my career. Both were athletes, young

SECTION 1: CONCLUSION

football players. I resonated with them, and you'll hear more about them in the next section.

I also realized I wanted more. I came from a background in coaching—I had spent a decade coaching. I was used to being around people, used to motivating, elevating, and making a difference. There was a void in my solo career. A real one. Looking back, I realize that all those years of coaching were preparing me for this next chapter. I didn't know it at the time.

I remember thinking, *Man, I just spent ten years coaching—did I waste that time?* Then I got into insurance. But now, almost ten years into the insurance industry, I look back and thank God for those coaching years. They prepared me to lead and support hundreds—soon to be thousands—of insurance agents across the country. Without that background in coaching, in leading and developing people from all walks of life, I don't think I'd be able to do what I'm doing today at this level.

One thing I always tell people is to reflect on their past. Your past creates you, prepares you, and *qualifies* you for what you're doing today.

So the key takeaways from Section 1 are that, to be a championship producer, you *need* to be sharply pointed. You *need* to reinvest. You *must* know your numbers. Those are the foundations.

Let's move on to building a championship *team*. It's something I look back on often—mentorship, community, and a lot of other things—but those two really stand out as I reflect on this journey and read through this section. The next half of this book is all about the transition. Maybe you're a solo producer, or you're running a small agency with one or two agents. Now you're ready to take it to the next level—to build a championship team.

For me, I wanted to build the New England Patriots or the Chicago Bulls of insurance. And that's exactly what we're doing right now: building a championship team on a foundation of

SECTION 1: CONCLUSION

culture, leadership, and community. Whatever you envision your dream team looking like, this next section is for you. It's about how to build that team, how to communicate your vision and mission, how to scale to new levels, and how to get comfortable with being uncomfortable.

I think of just this past week—we're constantly facing new breakpoints, new roadblocks. And when those moments of discomfort hit during growth phases, it's easy to want to retreat or curl up and hide. But I hope this next section prepares you for those moments. I want it to show you where the roadblocks might come, how to jump over them—or avoid them entirely. This section is about helping you build your dynasty—your own championship insurance team.

I also want to introduce my incredible wife, Emily Gruening, who joins us in this chapter. Emily brings over sixteen years of corporate experience to the table, having built her career at Ryman Hospitality Properties—a publicly traded hospitality and entertainment company behind some of the most iconic brands in the country, including the Grand Ole Opry, the Ryman Auditorium, Gaylord Hotels, and Ole Red.

As Director of Leadership and Training, Emily played a key role in developing internal training, leadership programs, and cultural systems that supported those brands. She focused on creating alignment between the employee experience, brand standards, and organizational growth—making sure the brand was as strong behind the scenes as it was on stage.

She joined our company as Chief of Operations—and was the *big grab* for our championship team. I always joke that I had to keep sweetening her signing bonus to get her to join us—but truly, she's the yin to my yang.

If there's one thing I've learned, it's that the foundation of building a championship team is having that incredible number two—someone who complements you, someone who helps you elevate. Emily fills the gaps where I'm weak. She's been a game-changer. We'll get into what our team looks like now, but I can't wait to introduce you to Emily and help you start building *your* championship team—your dream team, whatever that looks like.

So we'll see you in Section 2.

SECTION 2: BUILDING A CHAMPIONSHIP TEAM

As we get into Section 2, it's all about building a championship team. Everything we covered in Section 1 has been preparing you for this moment. You have to become a successful individual producer or a strong solo agency before you can build a true championship team.

What's exciting about this part of the book is that we're actively teaching this exact material right now in our Coach's Office program. Over the past few months, we've been working through much of this curriculum, so it's fresh—and I'm super excited to share it with you.

In this opening section, I want to give you a brief overview of what you're going to learn in Section 2. And I think one of the most important—yet most often overlooked—elements of building a championship team is laying the *foundation*: understanding what a championship team truly is at its core. Going back to the sports theme that runs through this book, I think of some of the greatest championship teams of all time—the Bulls with

Michael Jordan, the Patriots with Tom Brady, champions like Tiger Woods and Kobe Bryant. These teams and athletes had something in common: a clear vision, a defined mission, and a powerful strategy.

They built their own brand around *how* they achieved success—and it's no different in business or in building a championship insurance agency. You need a brand. You need a vision. You need a strategy to guide your team. That's exactly what we're going to focus on in this section: brand, vision, strategy, development, and culture.

Just this morning, I was on a call with our team, and we talked about how critical culture is—about the importance of having non-negotiables, core values, and a strong internal identity. In our agency, we emphasize recognition, which I believe is one of the most overlooked elements of team building. Everyone wants to feel valued. And recognition doesn't have to be monetary or tied to a trophy. It can be as simple as verbal appreciation. That kind of recognition is a cornerstone of culture.

We'll also dive into performance management—how to continually monitor, guide, and develop your team through a culture of accountability and support. And one of my favorite topics: how to find top talent. How do you attract it? How do you develop it? How do you get top-tier people to *want* to come work with you?

Another key area is training. How do you train a high-performing team and keep them consistent? When I was coaching successful sports teams, we trained *every single day*. It's no different in business. Training must be constant. You need a system that produces consistent results.

Leadership is another major focus. We've built a phenomenal leadership team. And in my opinion, a great leadership team is a reflection of your own weaknesses. You hire to fill your gaps. You surround yourself with leaders who are strong where you are not—and that's exactly what we've done.

Operational efficiency is next: what systems are you using? What systems should you be using? How do you select the right tools, implement them, and then optimize everything for peak performance? That's a massive part of building a championship team.

Then there's advanced sales and marketing. I talk about this a lot when I speak around the country. Too often, people put the cart before the horse. But here's the point: before anything else, you've got to dial in your internal systems. You've got to optimize your team, your sales processes, and your operations. *That's* what allows everything else to scale. And then we amplify that with marketing. First, we optimize—*then* we amplify. We never amplify something that hasn't been optimized. That's where so many people go wrong. They jump in and start spending a lot of money on marketing and advertising before they've optimized their systems. And in my opinion, that's a recipe for disaster.

Next, we discuss financial mastery. This is an area where I've really hired around my own weaknesses. How do we gain financial mastery over our numbers? How do we get the *right* information to make the *right* decisions? It's all about tracking the right metrics and using that data to drive your choices. Then there's client experience. How do we make our customers feel like they're getting a top-tier experience—like going to a Taylor Swift concert or a big-time event where they walk away thinking, *Wow, that was worth every penny*? That level of experience is what we want to deliver. From there, how do we scale? How do we take all these components—optimization, culture, leadership, financial mastery, client experience—and continue to innovate and adapt? Because if you're not constantly innovating and adapting, you're falling behind.

And finally, what's your exit plan? Do you want to leave a legacy? Do you have a succession plan? What does that look like for you? All of these components will be broken down in the next section. We're going to walk through them step by step and show you exactly how to build your championship team.

ONE
BUILD THE BRAND, BUILD THE BUZZ

As we get into the foundation—which, in my opinion, is brand, vision, and strategy—this really shifted for us when my wife, Emily, officially came on board in June 2024. She had always been involved in our agency and had already made a huge impact on our brand, vision, and strategy, but about eight months ago, we really began to amplify all of it.

I still remember meeting Emily back in 2018. With a big smile, my opening line was, "Holy dimples!" I quickly found out what she did for a living, and it was super cool—honestly, not a lot of people have a career like hers. She spent 16 years in hospitality, working with some of the most iconic brands in Nashville, Tennessee. As mentioned earlier, she was part of Ryman Hospitality Properties, which owns major hospitality and entertainment brands like the Ryman Auditorium, the Grand Ole Opry, the Gaylord Hotels, and well-known restaurants like Ole Red in downtown Nashville and beyond. She was incredibly passionate about her work, especially storytelling and elevating brands through training and development.

Emily brought a unique and powerful skill set to our agency, and she quickly started helping us develop our brand's mission, strategy, and vision. Over the course of a few years, we put together what I call her "sign-on package," and we were lucky enough to bring her on as our chief of operations. She's far more qualified than I am to speak on these topics, so without further ado, I'm excited to welcome Emily Gruening to this amazing book.

EMILY

Thank you, Chase, for that wonderful introduction. I'm extremely excited to be part of this, and truly, it's something Chase and I have built together over the last several years. As he said, I brought my skill set into the fold—focusing on our company's brand, collaborating on our internal culture, and beginning to intentionally shape what our organization stands for.

Even before we used that exact language, the foundation was already being laid. I remember we were right in the middle of COVID, which meant we had a lot of time together. That period really gave Chase space to start thinking differently about his agency. At the time, it was still called the Chase Gruening Agency—it was mostly just him, with a few agents showing interest in joining. But that's when the shift began. He said, "I want this to be about more than just me. I'm ready to rebrand this as a team." And that's exactly what we did—we rebranded the agency with a focus on culture, identity, and long-term growth.

The process came together in stages. I leaned into my background to think about both the tangible aspects—things like logo design, color palettes, and the overall brand story—and the intangibles: the kind of team we wanted to build and the kind of organization we wanted to become.

It wasn't until just over six months ago that I officially came on board full-time. I'd been playing a role in the agency's growth behind the scenes for years, but during that time, I was also continuing my career and wrapping up some major projects on the corporate side. When the timing aligned, I made the jump and joined the business fully. It's been an incredible experience so far—continuing the work we've done with Gruening Health & Wealth and launching COACHG. It's been a phenomenal ride, and I'm so excited for what's ahead. COACHG has truly been a ground-up experience for me—taking something from scratch and building it into what it is today has been incredibly special and a lot of fun. The second half of this book is all about taking that amazing thing you've built in your agency—whether you're still solo or beginning to grow a team—and scaling it beyond yourself. You might be reading this and already have a team in place, but maybe you haven't thought through some of these foundational components yet.

One of the most interesting things I've observed about people who continue to grow is that many never had the kind of leadership experience Chase had—working on a football team, coaching others, being led, and truly understanding leadership. For a lot of people, they jump straight into production. They're the ones executing. Then suddenly, they want to scale—but they've never really had the opportunity to stop and think about what it means to lead. They haven't been trained or gone through the formal experience of building and guiding a team. That's where this section becomes so valuable. It will walk you through the full life cycle of an agency—from building it from the ground up, to growing it, scaling it, and ultimately deciding what you want to do with it. We're excited to walk through that process with you—together.

Chase passed the baton to me for this first topic because I was fortunate enough to work with some truly remarkable brands. A few are now recognized nationwide, while others are rooted in Nashville and have been around for over a hundred years. I also had the opportunity to help launch new brands from the ground up. All of my experience was on the internal side—helping inspire people around the brand, maintain employee passion for it, and ultimately fuel its growth.

To me, a brand is just as powerful internally as it is externally. How you think about it, how you talk about it, how you live it within your team—it matters even *more* than the external perception. Because your people *are* your product. How your employees feel about your brand, and how they live out the brand promise, will ultimately shape the experience your clients have with it. So as I talk about branding, you'll notice that I focus heavily on the internal perspective.

Branding is the perception of your organization—its values, its identity, and its reputation, both inside and out. And for me, above all else, it's about *emotional connection*. It's the connection your employees feel. It's the connection you intentionally create with your clients and your broader audience. Why is that so important? Because branding builds trust. It builds recognition. And in a crowded market, you need to stand out. There are a lot of places people can go to get insurance. So what makes *you* different? What makes you different to work for? How do you create that emotional connection with your employees—who then, in turn, pass that connection along to your clients?

Where do you begin? Most people, ourselves included, when we started, automatically jumped to surface-level branding: "Let's change our name. Let's design a logo." That's where people usually want to start—the name, the visuals, the colors. But before you get there, there's some *internal* work that needs to happen—work that will set the foundation for everything else and make your name, logo, and branding efforts that much more meaningful. And that work starts with defining your mission and vision—internally. What is your mission? What is your vision for your organization? Once you're clear on that, everything else—your name, your logo, your colors, your message—can align with it and become that much more impactful. This is what ensures consistency, purpose, and clarity in how your brand presents itself. Most importantly, it gives both your team and your clients a clear understanding of what you're trying to accomplish—and what you stand for. That, I believe, is the most critical part: making sure everyone clearly understands your mission and that you're strong and consistent in communicating it.

In my previous career, this was one of the most important principles we upheld. We had to be absolutely clear on what we were trying to accomplish. Whether you were a steward in the kitchen or the newly appointed Chief Operating Officer, if you worked in one of our hotels, you sat through the same company orientation. You heard the same story about our mission, our vision, and our purpose. That experience taught me the value of making sure people form a strong emotional connection with the organization's mission right from the beginning.

For example, when I look at Gruening Health & Wealth, our mission focuses on education for the senior market. We emphasize the importance of educating and guiding clients so they can make informed decisions for themselves. That mission carries through both internally—with our team—and externally—with how we present ourselves to clients. Medicare and retirement planning are what we do, and we consistently reinforce that message to both employees and consumers. Once you define what you're trying to accomplish, it becomes much easier to refine other aspects of your brand.

The next step is identifying your target audience and making sure your brand speaks directly to them. It's interesting: when coaching different agencies, we often find that many have never taken the time to think deeply about this. Others have unintentionally pigeonholed themselves into a specific niche, only to realize it's not where they want to be. Taking a step back allows you to say, "Okay, I see how I ended up here, but my true target audience is actually over there—and I haven't done a good job aligning my branding or marketing to reflect that." Your brand needs to resonate with the people you most want to serve—those who are most likely to become loyal, long-term clients. Clarity around your target audience is absolutely essential. This is something we continue to define internally as well with COACHG. We spend a lot of time identifying which types of agents and agencies we know we can truly help. Being clear about that target audience is a crucial part of our own branding strategy.

Then there's your unique value proposition—what makes you different? This is the core of your differentiation strategy. Internally, it may inform how you hire and how you position yourself as an employer. Externally, it's the reason someone should choose you over the competition. It's the reason *you* believe you'll deliver the best possible experience. That unique value should be central to all of your branding efforts—from your messaging and marketing to how you lead your team and serve your clients.

And then we really get to the fun part. Once you've determined your mission, vision, and values, that work starts to guide your brand's *personality*. What's unique about my experience is that, while I've worked heavily on the internal side of branding, I see branding and culture as basically synonymous. For me, branding isn't just about visuals—it's about identity. I believe every brand has a personality, a story to tell, and a specific type of person it naturally attracts. Being thoughtful and consistent about that brand personality is what helps you build recognition and, more importantly, trust. When people who resonate with what you offer see your brand repeatedly, they begin to connect with it emotionally. They might think, *I keep seeing this, and it's something that intrigues me,* or *I love how fun, edgy, professional, or unique this brand feels.*

Brand personalities are fascinating. I often talk about the differences between Gruening Health & Wealth—our insurance agency—and COACHG, which helps agents and agencies grow. These two brands have very different personalities. That's obvious when you visit our websites, but it's also reflected in how we interact with clients. Every interaction, every piece of communication, is shaped by those defined brand identities. And we're intentional about it—we frequently say things like, *That doesn't align with our brand,* or *That's not the tone we're going for.* Knowing your brand personality and staying consistent with it is incredibly important.

Then, of course, come the visual branding elements. But by the time you get to visuals—your logo, your name, your brand colors—you've already done a lot of foundational work. Still, visual identity is the most immediate way your audience connects with your brand. When I've coached others through internal branding, I always say that your visual elements should reflect the personality of your brand.

Take Gruening Health & Wealth, for example; we have a clean, professional logo. Our color palette stands out, but it's polished. Our marketing materials, photos, and design choices all reflect a professional, trustworthy approach. On the other hand, COACHG has a more relaxed, approachable vibe. It feels cool, dynamic—like something you'd naturally gravitate toward if you were looking to amplify your business. It carries a sporty energy and a sense of momentum that really fits our mission there. So your visual elements should match the audience you're trying to reach and represent the essence of who you are. That includes things like your:

- **Name:** This evokes emotion and becomes the foundation of your brand. It's something you say and share every single day.
- **Logo:** The face of your brand. It's often the first impression people have of you and should be adaptable across different formats.

I was recently working with someone on her brand, and we were fine-tuning her visual identity. She printed her logo on a t-shirt and noticed that the words Senior Services—a key part of her business name—were too small compared to the rest of the logo, which featured her last name. She realized it just didn't work for her audience and market. And I told her, "That's a great insight." That kind of awareness is exactly what branding is all about. As you're working through these elements, these are the kinds of things you want to keep in mind. How will your brand translate across different media, formats, and sizes? In the example I mentioned earlier, we were able to catch an issue early—before the client went too far down a path and realized the problem too late.

Next, you want to create a strong, impactful tagline. How do you communicate your brand's mission and promise in a way that's clear and immediate—something people can grasp right away? For example, with Gruening Health & Wealth, our tagline is: *"Medicare and retirement planning. It's what we do."* It's extremely clear, and we use it everywhere. It helps our audience instantly understand what we're about.

Now, let's talk about color. Colors evoke emotion and carry subconscious associations, so it's important to choose ones that resonate with you and your brand personality. But beyond the selection itself, what really matters is *consistent* use. That's what builds recognition. When someone sees your colors, they should immediately think, *Oh, that's COACHG*, or *that's Gruening Health & Wealth*.

Fonts are another area that I'm really passionate about. Anyone who works with me knows how seriously I take font choices. Fonts are incredibly impactful. They affect readability and influence how your message is received. A clean, professional font communicates something very different from a playful or outdated one. For example, sometimes I see a font that reminds me of high school projects, and it instantly feels off-brand. Fonts contribute to how people perceive your brand, and when they're misaligned, it shows. They matter more than most people realize.

Then there's your brand voice and tone. This should align with your brand personality and be consistent across all your messaging. What you say—and how you say it—becomes your brand's identity in the eyes of your audience. Take time to hone that voice and make sure it reflects who you are and what you want your brand to be. All of these components—voice, visuals, fonts, colors—come together to create your brand's overall aesthetic. You want to document all of this clearly in your brand guidelines. Those guidelines should include:

- Your logo (and how and when to use it)
- Your fonts and type hierarchy
- Brand colors (with exact hex codes)
- Visual inspiration or sample photos
- Messaging tone and examples

Having this kind of brand toolkit is essential, especially if you're working with outside vendors or designers. You want them to understand exactly what your brand represents and to maintain consistency across everything they produce. All of these details will set you up for success from a branding perspective. They bring your brand to life—and just as importantly, they help you bring your employees along for the ride.

So, as you move from being an agency of one to building a team—or simply expanding your brand's presence in the market—be intentional. Revisit the basics:

- What's your mission and vision?
- Who is your target audience?
- How are you differentiating yourself?
- What's your brand personality?
- What do your visual brand elements say about your company?
- Are they consistent with your values and aspirations?

Make sure your overall aesthetic represents not just who you are today, but who you want to become in the future.

Once you've landed on all of those elements and thought them through, now it's time to launch—internally and externally. It's time to set the direction for where you're headed from here. You've built the vision—now the question becomes: How are you going to execute it? So I'm going to kick it back to Chase, who's going to dive into how to effectively and consistently communicate your vision to your team. How do you start to build a long-term strategic plan? How do you set actionable goals that will help you achieve that vision?

CHASE

One of the most important aspects of everything Emily just discussed is *how* we communicate it to our teams.

I say this all the time: You can be an amazing producer. You can be a top-level agent or a solo agency owner operating at a high level. But when you move to the next level—when you start building a *championship team*—communication becomes the key driver. That's what really moves the needle. How do you communicate your brand, your vision, and your strategy to your team? Some of the most important components include your communication style, how you motivate people, how you activate your team, and how you get everyone to buy into the brand's mission and vision. One thing we implemented in our company (which I'll go into more detail on in a later chapter) is splitting our company into 100 million shares.

We adopted a managing partner model where *every single employee* has equity ownership in the company. That model gives everyone a vested interest in our brand's success. It ties their daily work to the mission and makes them feel like owners—not just employees. Now, that's just one approach. There are many ways to communicate and reinforce your vision. But the point is this: to be an effective leader and build a true championship team, it's not just about what you *do*. It's about how you *communicate* your vision and how you *motivate* others to get on board with it. We've spent a lot of time internally developing how we communicate—what we share with our team, how we share it, and why it matters. That's a big part of our culture, and I'll dive deeper into that in the next chapter.

Now, let's talk about setting actionable goals because that's a critical part of executing your long-term strategy. Right now, our team has a big goal. We've rolled out a clear vision to reach a $100 million valuation within the next three to five years. But that starts with the question: What do we need to accomplish this year, in 2025, to make that possible? That's the short-term focus that leads to the long-term result. We've mapped out exactly how we're going to hit our 2025 (at time of writing) goals, and then we've shown the team what it will take to get there over the next five years. They can see the plan. They know what's required. And they know how their role fits into it. It's all laid out in front of them.

TWO
PROTECT THE LOCKER ROOM

In my opinion, there are two massive gaps in the insurance industry: leadership and culture. Having a phenomenal culture, attracting and developing top talent through that culture, and pairing it with a strong sales system—that's what sets great organizations apart. But for this chapter, we're focusing solely on culture.

Culture, as Emily mentioned earlier, is essentially your brand. It's what people think and feel when they hear your company name—whether it's COACHG, Gruening Health & Wealth, or whatever your brand may be. It's how people experience your business. In our company, we have a set of non-negotiables—core principles we do not deviate from. These are our pillars for success. They define what it means to be a part of our team.

As you read this, I encourage you to pause and ask yourself: *"What are my non-negotiables? What is the culture within my company?"* If you're a solo agent, now is the perfect time to start developing your culture. Define the values and behaviors that are essential to you. If you're leading a larger team, ask yourself: *"Have I clearly defined our culture? Do we have non-negotiables? Do we communicate them consistently?"* If not, now's the time to get those down—refine them and begin sharing them with your team.

Here are a few of our non-negotiables:

- **Always be growing:** Growth doesn't have to be 100% or 200% year-over-year, but we do need to be improving—both personally and professionally. We don't stay stagnant. We aim to be better than we were yesterday.
- **Show up:** Monday morning meetings at 8 a.m. Central are sacred. The entire team is there—on time, every week. We set the tone for the week. Likewise, my Coach's Office calls are always at noon Central on Mondays. Again, we start the week strong. It's a non-negotiable.
- **Communicate:** Communication is everything. A major rule for us: pick up the phone. So much gets lost in translation through text or email. When in doubt, call.
- **Be accountable:** To ourselves. To our teammates. To our goals—personal and collective. Accountability is foundational.
- **Respect each other:** No exceptions. Mutual respect is non-negotiable.
- **Family matters:** I know "family" is a buzzword in business these days, but for us, it's real. Our team feels like an extended family. Two of my greatest joys are being a husband and father. Right behind that is the honor of leading our team each and every week.

Our **values** build on that foundation. A few key ones:

Integrity

Do what you say. Do it the right way. Do it for the right reasons. And do it *consistently*.

Leadership

We must lead exceptionally. When I think back to the best sports teams I was ever part of, leadership wasn't just from the top—it came from within. We had captains, yes, but the whole team took ownership. And that's the model we strive to build. It was the seniors, the juniors, the freshmen—everyone on the team was a leader. Leadership existed at every level. And I see the same thing in our company. Within our culture, we have leaders beyond just our formal leadership team.

I want to touch on family again. It's something we preach within our organization, and it's something we truly practice. When I look back at the content we post daily across our social media platforms, it's interesting to see which pieces get the most engagement. One of the most popular clips out there right now is me talking about spending $30,000 to celebrate our team. And we did it again this year—only this time, we spent two to three times more, hosting a private event at the Bluebird Cafe in Nashville, just for our team. It was a night we'll never be able to recreate, but it was incredibly special—something we'll all remember. I'm a firm believer in celebrating our people and treating them like family.

Every year, we bring our entire team to our home. We hand out awards, bonuses, and recognition. We create moments that matter. We don't just talk about a family atmosphere—we live it.

And going back to that piece of content—it's telling that it resonated so widely. I think people are drawn to the idea of being valued. In today's business world, everything is focused on top-line profits and protecting the bottom line. But reinvesting in your people—your *family*—is one of the most powerful things you can do as a leader.

And that brings me to the next topic: *finding top talent*. You are a reflection of your team. I say it all the time. If you look at our team, it's filled with former athletes, coaches, and law enforcement professionals—people who are disciplined, motivated by structure, driven by recognition, and committed to being the best. Your culture and values will naturally attract the kind of people who align with them. And for us, that tends to be people who value discipline, purpose, and growth.

At many of the events I host, I speak on this exact topic. I'll often pick someone out from the audience and ask them, "What do you like to do in your spare time?" For me, it's sports. I was an athlete and a coach. Sports has always been part of my identity, and as a result, I attract people who share those values—competitors, high performers, team players.

I'll never forget Michael, a guy in the audience who said, "I like to fish." So I asked, "Do you have any fishing buddies? Do you know anyone in that circle who might be good at doing what you do?" I told him, "You should be out there *fishing for agents*," and everyone laughed. But the point is, you should look to lead people who you naturally connect with. As I've said before, you are most qualified to teach and lead *who you once were*—or even who you are today. So finding top talent starts with your non-negotiables, your values, and your identity. And when those are clear, the right people will be drawn to your culture.

Training

I'll let Emily speak more on this in a moment, but I want to emphasize that training is a huge part of your culture. How you train, how you lead, and how you develop your team, all speak volumes. As Emily mentioned earlier, in her former organization, it didn't matter if you were a C-suite executive or a cook in the kitchen—you went through the exact same onboarding process. Everyone, at every level, understood the company's vision, brand, mission, culture, and non-negotiables.

Ultimately, building a phenomenal culture comes down to leading by example. I always say: lead from the front. Many people work with us—or join The Coach's Office—because I'm out there actively doing what I teach. It's not that "do as I say, not as I do" mentality. I'm literally doing as I say—every single day. And that carries weight. It attracts people who want to be part of something authentic. So ask yourself: *"Am I leading by example? Am I willing to step in and lead from the front when things aren't going smoothly?"*

Performance management is another crucial part of culture. We touched on it earlier, but it deserves a deeper look. We regularly meet with every member of our team—whether that's weekly or bi-weekly—and that includes our administrative staff. We conduct performance reviews to understand where each person is thriving, where they're struggling, and how we can support them. We do this with our agents too. We help them identify areas for optimization and growth, and we hold them accountable to the goals they've set for themselves. I know the term "performance management" can sound a bit corporate, but at the end of the day, it's about accountability and support. Are we helping our team members reach their goals? That's what matters most.

Rewards and recognition are also foundational. I've talked about spending $30,000 to $50,000 on our team events—but at the core of it, it's not just about the money. It's about celebrating our people. It's about showing appreciation and creating experiences that make them feel seen, valued, and connected to something greater. For our team, it's not just about the bonuses and awards. It's about being part of a family. Being part of a mission. Feeling like they're contributing to something bigger than themselves.

I've heard it said that your company's mission should be so big that everyone else's individual goals can fit inside of it. And I really believe that's what we've built—a vision and a mission so meaningful that it provides space for everyone to grow, thrive, and succeed. That's when you know you've created something special. So, with that, I want to bring in Emily to close this chapter. She's been instrumental in helping me shape much of this. Just last night, she was reading a book on culture, and I asked her, "If you could write a book on anything, what would it be?" And without hesitation, she said: *Culture*. So here's Emily with a few final thoughts.

EMILY

When you think about culture, it really boils down to this: How do we do things around here? Culture is the playbook for your organization. It's a shared set of beliefs and values. It's leadership consistency. It's the clearly defined expectations you set for how you serve your clients—and each other. And it's the heart of your company's mission. And all of that matters, for a lot of reasons.

It's going to help you, as a leader, drive your decision-making —especially if you've clearly communicated how things are done, the values you uphold, and the expectations you've set. That clarity becomes critical when things get tough. And they will. Or when things go really well, and you want to celebrate a major win, your values become the lens through which you decide how to respond. For example, one of our core values at Gruening Health & Wealth is performance: we play to win. At the beginning of each year, we host a weekend summit to celebrate the previous year's wins and to declare our goals and performance expectations for the year ahead. It's one of our team's favorite events, and we work hard to make it feel special. On the flip side, we've also had to make tough personnel decisions because of our value of accountability. We know that if we don't hold everyone to the same standard, we risk unraveling the culture and progress we've worked so hard to build.

Your values also help guide the behavior you're looking for from your team and align everyone around a common purpose. At the end of the day, people want to belong. They want to feel purpose. They want to be part of a winning team. And that's really what we're here to help you do—build your championship team. That desire to be part of something meaningful and successful is at the top of most people's lists. And as a leader, you need to understand that every organization *has* a culture, whether you're intentional about it or not. The best cultures don't happen by accident. They're built on purpose, with intention. They're created by leaders who define what they want their culture to be, communicate it clearly, live it consistently, and hold others to that same standard. Because either way, you're going to end up with a culture —it just may not be the one you *meant* to create. So define it. Communicate it. Live it. And expect others to do the same.

THREE
LEAD FROM THE FRONT

I'm really passionate about leadership. As I mentioned earlier, I believe it's one of the biggest gaps on many teams. You can build a successful solo agency without being a phenomenal leader. You can get away with being the top producer, running things on your own. But when it comes to building a team? That's where a lot of people struggle—because they lack leadership.

If that statement makes you feel a little uncomfortable—if you're thinking, *I'm a good leader, he doesn't know what he's talking about*—well, that might be a sign you've got leadership gaps to work on. I promise you that if you feel defensive about your leadership, there's room for growth. I remember talking to a few agents who said things like, "Yeah, so-and-so left me, but they sucked," or "They weren't making the calls," or "They left because of [XYZ]."

But back when I was coaching, there was a saying I lived by: *If you're allowing it, you're coaching it.* In other words, if something's going wrong on your team and you're not addressing it, you're silently endorsing it. As leaders, we are ultimately responsible for what's happening in our organizations. If you haven't taught someone the right way, if you don't have systems in place, if you're not clearly leading—then your team is set up to fail.

There are a ton of phenomenal *players*—people who are excellent at what they do. We've got amazing producers on our insurance team. But many of them will be the first to tell you—they're not ready for leadership. And that's okay. There's a big difference between being an incredible player and being an incredible coach. Lots of people can *do* the work—but can they *teach* it? Can they *lead* others through it? That's where the real growth happens. That's where the big impact—and the long-term success—comes from. And yes, there's a roadmap to becoming a phenomenal leader.

We've already touched on the first step: defining your leadership culture. What are your non-negotiables? What do you stand for? Once you've defined that, the next step is building an *organizational structure*. This was something we lacked in the early days. I used to be the CEO—and the head coach—and I had fifteen people reporting directly to me. That's not sustainable. Think about a championship football team. You've got the head coach, then coordinators, and then players. The coordinators report to the head coach, and the players report to the coordinators. The head coach still leads the whole team, but there's a clear structure that allows each leader to do their job effectively.

We've now built that same type of structure into our company. On the following pages, we'll include an overview of what our current structure looks like. Here's how we've set it up: At the top, we have the CEO. Directly under the CEO is the leadership team. Each department or team member reports to a specific leader on that leadership team. I now have only three direct reports—each of whom oversees their own teams. And within those teams, there are more leaders. It's a layered system designed to empower leadership at every level.

I encourage you to pause here and do an exercise: Write down your *current* organizational structure. Then write down your *ideal* structure—what you'd like it to look like. That simple comparison—current vs. desired—gives you a clear roadmap. You'll see exactly where you are and where you want to go. And then you can begin figuring out how to bridge that gap. Put it down on paper. See it in front of you. That's the first step toward building a leadership-driven organization.

And, as always, lead from the front. I can't say that enough. Exceptional leaders lead from the front. They have a demonstrated capacity—they can teach because they've done it. They don't just talk the talk; they walk the walk. For me, that's been one of the key factors in attracting top leaders. When I speak to someone about joining our team, I wear the hat they're wearing. I've been in their shoes. I've faced the same struggles. And that connection makes a major difference—not just in attracting top talent, but also in motivating and developing them. I believe you're uniquely qualified to lead the people who resonate with your leadership style. For me, as a former coach, I naturally connect with athletes and high performers. That shared mindset creates a foundation for mutual trust and growth.

Leadership isn't just about doing the work—it's about coaching, mentoring, and developing others. Can you develop people? I think of Travis Goviea, our national sales director. He's been with me since day one. His growth over the past decade has been phenomenal. He started as an individual producer, moved into a sales manager role, and is now leading on a national level. Each step in that journey brought its own challenges—and with every promotion came new growth opportunities. As leaders, our job is to guide and support that process. We're not just here to hire talent; we're here to develop and elevate it.

And that's not just theory—it's personal. Throughout this

journey of building a championship insurance team, I've faced plenty of roadblocks. I've hit speed bumps. And I've been fortunate to have people who coached, mentored, and developed me. That's what real leadership is about—lifting others while continuing to grow yourself.

So, the question becomes: Can you bring on leadership? Can you attract top talent? But more importantly—can you develop them? Can you help your people see a clear path for growth and provide them with the tools, mentorship, and structure to get there? We've built systems to support this. One example is our annual goal-planning process. We help team members define their big-picture goals—and then we meet bi-weekly or monthly to track progress. We ask: "Are we hitting the benchmarks that move us toward that big goal?" Because let's face it—having a big goal is great. But how are you tracking your progress? How are you holding people accountable for it?

Leadership is something I'm deeply passionate about. It's one of the most overlooked areas of building a truly exceptional company. If you want to scale, if you want to reach the $100 million valuation level—you can't do it alone. You need to become a leader who develops leaders. And this is where Emily and I both share a unique passion. She brings a completely different background, shaped by years in corporate leadership and development. Her experience gives her a powerful perspective on what leadership looks like in larger, more structured organizations. So with that, I'd love for Emily to share her insight on this topic.

EMILY

Leadership has been a huge part of my career for many years. My role focused on leadership development—coaching and supporting leaders across the organization so they could be more effective and successful in leading their teams. And while I was coaching others, I was also learning how to lead myself—which, let's be honest, is still a work in progress. I really believe that leadership is always a work in progress. It evolves with every team, every challenge, and every season of your life.

One thing I used to share in leadership training sessions—and it always surprised people—is this: Statistically, the average person is promoted into their first leadership role around the age of thirty. But they don't receive formal leadership training until they're about forty-two. That's a twelve-year gap. So, for over a decade, people are leading teams—learning on the fly, often without tools or training—and that can create a huge gap in effectiveness, culture, and consistency. So, there's this twelve-year gap where many new leaders are essentially fumbling through, figuring things out as they go.

And as Chase mentioned earlier, it comes back to the difference between playing and coaching. In many organizations, you'll often see the top server, the best accountant, or the highest-performing individual contributor suddenly promoted into a leadership role. The assumption is, "They're great at what they do—so they must be ready to lead." But the truth is, the skills needed to excel in a role are very different from the skills required to lead people. Leading people is an entirely different skill set—one that often hasn't been tapped into or developed in that previous role.

For many of you reading this, you've been solo producers. You've been focused on building your personal book of business and driving your own success. Now, you're ready to scale by adding people to your team. That shift requires more than just expanding your business—it requires developing yourself as a leader and, more importantly, redefining your role in the process. Leadership begins with self-awareness—understanding your strengths, recognizing your growth areas, and being open to learning. Don't assume you already have all the answers. Leadership isn't one-size-fits-all. It's subjective. It's emotional. You're dealing with people—their highs and lows, their struggles and successes. You're not just a boss. You're a mentor. A coach. A guide. And you need tools to help you lead through all of that.

I also want to emphasize the power of coaching, mentoring, and people development. This is where the culture you're building —one that you've been so intentional about—really comes to life. Because when you invest in your people, when you genuinely have their best interests at heart, that culture becomes tangible. Consistent one-on-ones, knowing what your team members' goals are, and working with them on personal development plans— these are the habits that help people grow. And when you grow your people, you grow your business.

This also creates a strong balance between hiring top external talent and developing your internal team. Something I always used to say when coaching and leading my own teams is this: the beauty of promoting from within is that you already know what you're getting. You know someone's strengths. You know their challenges. You know what they need to work on and where they shine. Sometimes, leaders hesitate to promote from within because they're too focused on what someone isn't ready for. Meanwhile, they'll bring in an external hire with a great résumé who says all the right things—but who hasn't been tested within your culture. That external person might bring a lot of value—but you don't really know all sides of them. And sometimes, you see things you didn't expect. Don't underestimate the value of knowing what you're getting when you develop and promote from within. It can do wonders for your culture when you take someone from the ground up and bring them along for the journey.

To close, I'd just say this: Be open. Understand that leadership is a constant work in progress. Don't be too hard on yourself. Be authentic. And take the time to clearly define the leadership qualities and values that matter to *you*—especially as you bring other leaders into your organization and expand your structure. Doing so will help you set clear expectations and create a leadership culture with consistency and purpose across your team.

FOUR
PRACTICE LIKE YOU PLAY

When it comes to building a championship team, training has to be a priority. In fact, we were just talking about this on our Monday non-negotiable call this morning. And you've heard me say this analogy over and over—but it's worth repeating until it sticks: Championship teams train every single day. Now, I'm not asking you to train every single day, but I am asking you to train every single week—multiple times.

How do you train your team every week? For us, we offer four training opportunities every day for our internal team. One of them is our national call, which we call "The Huddle"—this is where we welcome producers from across the country inside the COACHG platform. In addition to that, we host three internal training sessions and a fourth hybrid session, for a total of four trainings per week focused on sales, product knowledge, and developing your sales system. And that's exactly what our sales team needs. So I can't stress this enough: you must have a training platform or program laid out for your team. A lot of times I talk to agents and agency owners in the COACHG platform, and one of the biggest things they should be doing is designing their own internal training systems—something that grows with their agency.

Training isn't something you did. Training is something you do. That's what we preach, teach, and coach every single day. I'll break down exactly how we train in just a second, but the main takeaway here is this: training drives accountability. If you don't have consistent training, you won't have consistent results.

Inconsistent training = inconsistent processes = inconsistent outcomes.

Training builds accountability and consistency. And when you're scaling and growing, those are two things you need more than anything. You want your business to be predictable. You want to understand your growth metrics clearly—not just guess your way through it. That's why it's crucial to have a well-structured, intentional training program. Like I said, for us, it's five sessions per week.

As a leader, you have to be involved. You don't have to run every session, but you should be plugged in. Personally, I host at least one training session each week. I stay involved—as the CEO, as the head coach—because I believe in leading from the front. My sessions are typically higher level, focused on motivation, vision, and communication—helping the team understand why we do things and what we're focusing on that week. We take a very hands-on approach. We host in-person boot camps, in-person trainings, virtual Zoom trainings, and weekly hands-on sessions run by our leadership team.

Chuck McDowell is the founder of the world's largest timeshare exit team, doing over $100 million in annual revenue. Chuck said, "Inspect what you expect." That's such a powerful mindset.

It's not just *do as I say*—it's *do as I do*. We need to regularly inspect what we expect from our team. We need to lead by example, track results, and codify our systems so we can repeat and scale them.

So how do we do that? Well, it starts with Rookie Season—COACHG's entry-level module series and foundational training track. I often describe Rookie Season as our entry-level course—or a training designed for someone looking to optimize their sales process or new agent needing to be trained from the ground up. When a new agent joins our organization, we plug them directly into this program. And it's not just for our internal team—agents from all over the country also join and benefit from it.

Rookie Season offers a systemized approach to sales training. It teaches agents how to:

- Become an Agent of Interest
- Prospect and lead gen
- Effectively run an appointment
- Communicate clearly and confidently
- Handle objections
- Present Medicare and retirement planning
- Transition smoothly during the sales process
- Complete applications efficiently
- Deliver an outstanding customer experience

It's a foundational course—an essential starting point. From there, we pair it with live weekly trainings and coaching calls, where we help agents work through any specific areas they're struggling with as they move through the course material.

As I reflect on my years of coaching, one thing stands out: every individual learns differently. Some players pick things up immediately. I think of Travis Goveia—he's now one of our leaders, and I coached him back when he played football at Millikin

University. He barely needed coaching—he just got it. There are players who make you look good because they're naturally gifted. But others need more support.

One that comes to mind is Ron Smith. I love the guy—he's like a little brother to me. And he needed more hand-holding in the beginning. He was a different kind of learner. But now? He's a top-tier agent with a bright future.

That's what being a great leader and trainer is all about—recognizing that not everyone learns the same way. While you need a consistent training process, how you help individuals understand and fit into that process is where the magic happens. It's in the customization, the tweaks, and yes, sometimes the hand-holding, that real development takes place. While we use Rookie Season as the foundational system, we understand that every person requires personalized support to fully integrate into it.

Now, let's talk about our advanced trainings—Two-Point Plays. A lot of agents and agencies come to us specifically because of this powerful sales system. We call it Two-Point Plays because it's based on the football concept of a two-point conversion—strategic plays designed to add extra value. These aren't trick plays. They're planned, practiced, and purposeful. Most people don't realize that football teams have three, four, or five specific two-point plays they practice every single week. They're very intentional. And we apply that same principle to our sales approach.

The Two-Point Plays system is a codified, systematic method for uncovering hidden exposures and identifying additional opportunities within a client's situation. It helps agents bring those exposures to light and provide real solutions through:

- Cross-selling
- Packaging additional policies
- Customizing coverage based on client needs
- Embedding throughout a systematic sales process

We teach agents how to embed and present solutions like cancer, heart attack, and stroke policies, home care, recovery and skilled care, annuities, dental, hospital indemnity, and more. The idea is to take a traditional appointment and turn it into a comprehensive planning session—helping clients cover multiple exposures and significantly increasing the agent's first-year commission.

So, that's how we train. We build proven courses and systems that not only train our internal team, but are also taught to agents and agencies nationwide. These are repeatable, scalable, and rooted in real-world success. They've become our standard operating procedures—our SOPs.

I'll be the first to admit, when I first heard the term, I had no idea what it stood for. It sounded like something technical, something over my head. But then Emily came into our organization and introduced us to SOPs, and now I'm convinced they're absolutely essential. So, I'm going to kick this over to Emily to dive into SOPs and all things training.

EMILY

Looking at everything we've talked through so far—you've taken the time to define your culture, clarify who you want to be, and what you want to accomplish. You've put in the effort to find top talent, engage them, and bring them on board with excitement and energy. Now comes the moment to put your money where your mouth is.

How you onboard and train a new employee creates the very first impression of what their career will be like in your organization. And that impression matters. It's critical to be prepared when someone new joins your team. Make sure they're trained, supported, and truly ready to go. It's tempting—especially during busy seasons or when you're short on time—to cut corners. You might think, *We've got a ton of leads coming in*, or *It's AEP, and things are crazy. Let's just fast-track this. They'll figure it out.* But when you do that, you're putting both them—and yourself—at a disadvantage. Skipping proper onboarding and training may save time in the short term, but it often creates long-term issues that are far more costly. So do right by your business—and by your people—by taking the time to set them up for success.

Give them a strong, intentional first impression. Set clear expectations. Provide clarity on their role and what success looks like. One of the most important things you can do in onboarding is simply tell people what you expect. That alone provides a path forward. For example, we just onboarded a new administrative assistant at Gruening Health & Wealth. I had a day-by-day, hour-by-hour agenda prepared for her first couple of weeks. She had a checklist of everything she needed to learn and feel confident about. I scheduled time for her to be trained on each of those items—and then we regrouped to review how she was doing with each one. The point is that even if you can't be the one doing the training yourself (because, let's be honest, you're probably wearing a lot of hats), you can still own the process. You can make sure the right training is happening, and that your new hire is getting exactly what they need.

And that brings us to what Chase mentioned earlier—SOPs. At the end of the day, SOPs are about consistency in your brand and business. You want to know that processes are being done the same way across the board—whether it's your administrative team, your agents, or your leadership team. That's how you ensure high-quality, repeatable outcomes. SOPs and training manuals provide clarity. They help everyone understand what to do, how to do it, and why it matters. We've built SOPs for both our agent side and our administrative side—and as we continue growing our leadership team beyond just Chase and me, we're developing more every step of the way.

It can be easy to shortchange onboarding and training. But if you do it well—and with intention—you set your team and your company up for incredible success.

CHASE

When it comes to agents, our standard operating procedures are built around the client needs assessment (CNA), the flow chart, and the intake form. Let's break each one down:

Client Needs Assessment (CNA)

The CNA is exactly what it sounds like—a client needs assessment. It's our starting point. It's the guide for every single conversation we have with a new client. Think of it like going to the doctor. Before making any recommendations, a doctor asks you a handful of questions. The CNA works the same way. It gives you permission to ask important, relevant questions, uncover exposures, and ultimately embed multiple policies that increase first-year commission. It's your foundation.

Flow Chart

This one has a fun origin. I had an agent come to me once and say, "Chase, I've been listening to everything you're teaching, and I wanted to put it into a flow chart. If someone can make it through this chart, they've had a great appointment." That agent—Wes—was spot on. So we developed it. The flow chart is basically a checklist. If you can check every box, you've had a phenomenal appointment. It's that simple. And yes—you can download it for free at coachghuddle.com. I promise it'll become one of your favorite tools.

Intake Form

The intake form is quick and simple. It helps you collect client information so you can input the data later without disrupting the flow of your appointment. It keeps things clean, clear, and efficient. These three tools—CNA, flow chart, and intake form—are the go-to SOPs we use and recommend for every agent. They bring clarity, consistency, and confidence to your appointments.

Conclusion

If you take one thing away from this chapter, let it be this: Ongoing training is the most important thing you can do. At The Coach's Office, that's our core philosophy. It's what we preach, teach, and coach. We host The Huddle every week. We offer Game Plan sessions every week. That means agents get to train weekly. Leaders get to develop weekly. Owners get to grow their teams weekly. These are two things I'm deeply passionate about. Two things we've brought to the market in a big way. And two things I believe will be standard in our industry in the future.

FIVE
TIGHTEN THE PLAYBOOK

As you grow your championship team, operational efficiency becomes an absolutely critical focus—and one of the biggest drivers of real progress in your agency or business. Earlier, I talked about the importance of building an organizational chart. Start with where you are right now. Maybe that's just you—and that's perfectly okay. But on the other side of that page, draw what your aspirational organizational chart looks like. Where do you want to go? Who do you want on your team?

For us, there was a time when we were stuck in the middle. We had an organizational chart, but it was disorganized. At one point, I had fifteen to twenty people reporting directly to me. Let me tell you—that's not a fun place to be. Having ten, twenty, or thirty people reporting to you? That's not growth—that's misery. Right now, our operational organizational chart has three people reporting directly to me: our director of business development, our National sales director, and Emily, our chief of operations. Beneath each of them—our leadership team—are their respective departments, each involving many people. This structure has really streamlined things at the top. It allows me to focus on communicating with just three people and frees up my time so our leadership team can do what they do best—things that are, frankly, not my strengths.

Having a clear organizational chart has been incredibly important. The most important part of it, in my opinion, is that it allows people to see where they can grow. An organizational chart is really a ladder of ascension. It motivates your employees by giving them a clear vision of where they can go. It gives them something to strive for. And I think when you can see it, touch it, feel it—it's right there in front of you—it really helps you kick into overdrive and go after what's next. So I believe it's extremely important in streamlining your agency's processes. It took me a long time to discover that. Finding the right people—the "whos" who were already doing things really well—and learning from them helped me streamline some things in my own organization.

And here's something important to understand: let's use football as an example. A lot of times, as coaches, we move players around to different positions as we get to know them and understand their talents and strengths. Many kids come in wanting to be the quarterback. But I'll tell you right now, a lot of them aren't cut out to be quarterbacks. I'm not very tall, and I can't throw a football to save my life. I was a nose guard (right in the middle of that defensive line), and it didn't take long to figure that out.

But for a lot of kids—and coaches—it takes trial and error to figure out where someone fits best on a team. It's no different in a business or insurance agency: you have to use your people effectively. For example, our director of business development, Chris, came to us with a strong corporate background in business and finance. To have him just working as a sales agent would not have fully utilized his talents. Elevating him to director of business development allowed him to oversee our external partnerships and help optimize and streamline their agencies. He brings a business-minded, operational perspective and essentially acts as a fractional COO for our partners. That's where his strengths lie—leading from a business and operational standpoint, and ultimately helping us recruit and develop other agents. He can sell at a high level, no doubt, but we're maximizing both his value and our business by putting him in the right role.

Travis, for another example, is our national sales director. He's one of the best I've seen when it comes to teaching, training, and coaching new agents. If he were just selling, we'd be missing out. What he truly excels at is teaching others how to sell. And what I learned quickly is that if you can teach 10, 20, 30 people to sell even 50% as well as you can, that's a whole lot more than what you could do alone. So Travis's strengths are best used by developing other agents into top producers. In turn, we get a lot more production by using his strengths correctly.

Emily—my wife—isn't even licensed, and she shouldn't be, because her strengths lie in operations. If I put her in a sales role, I can already picture it—she'd be cringing trying to sell insurance. We knew that from the start. It was pretty obvious. Her strengths are in developing a phenomenal brand, telling our story through that brand, and building an incredible culture and training system.

Our leadership team is highly effective in their roles. Our job was to identify what suited each person best, create those positions, and essentially focus on their strengths—then surround ourselves with people who are strong in their respective roles.

When it comes to agents, I have a very firm philosophy: your sales agents should do absolutely nothing besides sell. One of the most overlooked issues is that many agents wear 600 different hats. They're the admin, the accountant, the processor—they're even the ones calling the companies. None of that generates revenue. So we have to hire people around them to provide support. All they should be doing is selling. If someone on our sales team is doing anything other than selling, they know that's one of my biggest pet peeves. As agents, we don't do anything but sell. And if someone is, they need to tell me so I can find someone—or create a position—to take that off their plate. Agents must stay focused solely on sales.

Our administrative team handles everything else. In our operation, we have about four administrative positions, and they are the lifeblood of what we do. They take non-revenue-generating tasks off our plates so we can focus on bringing in revenue. Our leadership team and agents are all positioned to generate revenue within their departments. The admin team handles everything else. That's one of the most overlooked and underappreciated aspects—these roles should actually make you money. If you're hiring administrative staff that gives you time back and removes tasks that don't generate revenue, then you're actually increasing your company's revenue and optimizing operations. When you hire effectively and streamline processes, it makes you money.

The hardest part for me has been growing into a much larger payroll. We now have several leadership positions earning six-figure base salaries plus commission. Our agents are six-figure earners. Our administrative staff is paid above industry standards. And I'm really proud of that. I believe it's a big reason why we're running so efficiently. With what I would consider a small internal team, we're achieving big numbers. I attribute that to our agency's streamlined processes—and the role that technology and automation tools play. I'll be the first to admit that this used to be an uncomfortable area for me. But once we brought in automations—webinars, landing pages, online funnels—it changed the game.

Again, the key is to think of it as buying back your time. How can we automate tasks that generate revenue even while we sleep? We have thousands of people engaging with our online educational touchpoints every week—and they're all automated. While our team is out generating new business, our funnels and automation tools are doing the work in the background. This technology and automation—while it can be expensive and sometimes uncomfortable—ultimately ties back into operational efficiency. When you find the right technology, the right automation tools, and the right systems, it's actually making you money.

This is a hot topic during our Coach's Office Game Plan calls. Every single week, someone asks me, "What do you use for this?" or "How do you streamline that?" My answer is that there are a lot of different tools, programs, and software options out there. The key is finding the *whos*—the people doing exactly what you want to do—and learning from them and their systems. That's exactly what we've created: a platform where you can discover the best systems and see what's really working for others.

EMILY

When I think about summarizing this chapter and some of the things Chase talked about, I reflect on my experience watching people in the hospitality industry move from line-level roles into leadership positions. Similarly, many of you are transitioning from being the sole agent in your business to looking at how to scale and build a team beneath you. It's about taking the time to focus on working *on* the business, not just *in* the business. So many people are used to being in the weeds, doing all the things themselves, and find it challenging to delegate. But as you continue to grow, it becomes essential—just as Chase mentioned—to bring additional people on board so you can free up your time, work on the business, and stay ahead of trends by creating efficiencies.

This is such an important part of the process—and one that took me a long time to learn in my own career. It's hard to let go of the things you've built and are so passionate about. But remember: if you don't, you're holding yourself and your organization back. Ultimately, it's about giving yourself the space and time to truly lead your business and make the changes needed to scale effectively.

SIX
CALL THE PERFECT PLAY

As we get into advanced sales and marketing, this is where—at least in my opinion—the big leagues begin. When it comes to this level of strategy, we're thinking in terms of the power of the many through the one. What is the one thing I can do that creates massive amounts of leads or opportunities in a single setting or through a single effort? A few game-changing ideas come to mind, and one of the biggest for us has been strategic partnerships. In my view, to land those high-level strategic partnerships, you need a team. If you want a partnership that brings in 1,000, 2,000, or even 3,000 leads or customers a year, you need the infrastructure and support in place to handle that kind of volume. For us, we've had major hospital partnerships come alongside us. We've also partnered with large insurance agencies—agencies with 100,000+ policyholders. And those opportunities have come our way largely due to the size and scope of our team, the support we can offer, and the way we've branded ourselves in local markets.

When it comes to advanced sales and marketing strategies, I place partnerships at the top of the list because they cost you nothing—but can give you everything. As you're working through this, ask yourself: *"What costs me nothing but can bring huge returns?"* That's likely your biggest opportunity. If you're looking to scale without increasing overhead, landing big-time partnerships is how you play in the big leagues. So how do you do that? It goes back to the who. For me, every one of these relationships came from people—people I already knew within those organizations, or people who knew someone and made an introduction. It all starts with relationships: putting yourself out there, taking a chance, getting the first meeting, and having real conversations about the value you bring to the table in exchange for your services.

I'd encourage you to pause and write down potential partnerships in your area. Maybe you don't yet have the team to support big ones—that's fine. Start with what you can go after now, and make another list of aspirational partnerships for the future. It could be a local insurance agency or financial advisor you can partner with. Over time, you can target major hospitals, national insurance agencies, or large HR departments. That's the kind of opportunity we're talking about.

Next up is one of our biggest investments: building proven marketing funnels and sales systems. In The Coach's Office, we teach exactly how to build these funnels and systems. At the time of writing this, we're spending anywhere from $10,000 to $20,000 per week on paid ads and online marketing. In return, we're generating a significant volume of leads. For example, we typically receive around 1,000–2,000 registrations per week across our webinars, seminars, and other educational touchpoints. That's 1,000 + leads weekly, driven by paid ads and optimized funnels. In my opinion, this is one of the first areas you need to optimize.

We talk a lot about training, sales skills, and first-year commission per client and ROAS. If we go back to that concept, first-year commission per client and ROAs are the most important metrics to help you decide whether you're ready to invest in large-scale sales funnels. Again, this is something we teach and something I'm very passionate about—but I'll tell you right now, not everyone is ready for it.

We cannot put the cart before the horse when it comes to leveraging digital marketing and social media. We touched on digital marketing earlier, but it's worth emphasizing. There are many people out there—unfortunately, we're not one of them—who have zero marketing costs because they've built phenomenal social media channels that bring in leads organically. Two names that come to mind are Chris Westfall and Matt Clauson. If you look up their YouTube channels, you'll see they each have over 100,000 followers. They don't spend a dime on marketing. They've created these powerful lead-generating machines just by consistently posting videos over time. Their channels have blown up and now bring in tons of leads.

You can absolutely leverage social media, YouTube, and other platforms to generate leads. For us, we've been building our social media presence for over a decade, and while we're not seeing YouTube-level numbers, we've definitely converted free posts into real sales and revenue. Right now, we have a dedicated social media team. They post on five platforms—twice a day, seven days a week. That consistent messaging builds brand awareness, creates leads, and increases frequency. So continue to leverage digital marketing and social media—and as your team grows, invest in those channels.

Just because it's a free lead source doesn't mean you should be the one managing it. The leads themselves might not cost anything, but buy your time back by having someone else handle it. That's one of the biggest lessons I've learned. I used to do it all

—posting, managing the platforms—but now I don't touch it. I've delegated it, and that's allowed us to scale.

The ultimate goal with advanced sales and marketing is to create order-takers within your organization. The ideal scenario is that a client comes to one of our team members and simply says, "Hey, I want [XYZ]"—and our agent makes the sale. They look like rockstars, but really, it's the automation and advanced sales and marketing behind the scenes that create what we call an "order taker." And if you can build an organization with 100 order takers—well, I'll see you at the beach one day.

Let's talk about intentional congruency. All of these strategies need to work together. We literally draw a circle in the middle of a page and put order takers in the center—that's the goal. Then we ask, "What are all the things that lead to creating an order taker?" Sales funnels, digital and social media, strategic partnerships, brand frequency—these all contribute. You could also just write advanced sales and marketing in that center circle. The point is that all of these components are deeply interconnected. When I develop advanced strategies, I look for congruency. Every piece of our marketing—from billboards to TV ads, commercials, newspapers, radio, online campaigns—they all work together. That's intentional congruency. It's about deliberately placing these touchpoints in the marketplace so that the combined frequency leads to revenue.

And that's the key: frequency. We touched on it earlier, and it's worth repeating. How many different times—and in how many different ways—can we touch our potential consumers? I see it all the time. Someone will say, "I saw you on a billboard, then I saw you on TV, and then an ad popped up on social media—and I just thought, *I've got to talk to these guys.*" It's often a combination of different advanced marketing and sales touchpoints that leads to a sale—and more importantly, it's the frequency of those touchpoints.

If we were to put that into a formula, it would be:

Marketing types + Frequency = Sale

EMILY

From my perspective, I want to go back to the first chapter in this section, where we talked about branding. This is where that branding piece becomes so important—defining your logo, your colors, and your messaging. As Chase mentioned, the more avenues and platforms you use, the more exposure you get, and the more important consistency becomes. You want people to recognize you across all platforms, and that only happens when your brand is consistent. So keep that in mind when you're creating your brand. Ask yourself: *"What would this look like on a billboard? On TV?"* That exercise can help guide you toward what feels right for your business and brand identity.

The clearer and more consistent your brand is, the more confident and scalable your marketing becomes. All of that contributes to building trust and credibility. When your branding is consistent and professional, people start to feel like they know you—even before they've ever interacted with your organization. That sense of familiarity builds confidence and naturally leads to conversion. Whether they see you on social media, on a billboard in town, or even eventually on TV—they're starting to trust you. And your brand delivers that message before you even say a word.

SEVEN
WIN THE FANS

This next chapter focuses on the client experience—and how to make it excellent. When I think back on some of the great experiences I've had in my life, one that really stands out happened right here in Nashville, Tennessee. The Taylor Swift craze was in full swing, and my wife happened to score last-minute tickets to her concert. We didn't pay outrageous prices—just $200 or $250 a ticket—so we jumped on it and went. I remember wearing my Titans jersey, thinking I was being funny and trying to blend in with the crowd.

Long story short, the experience was *incredible*. I wasn't a huge Taylor Swift fan going in, and I didn't have a lot of expectations, but it was amazing to see 70,000 people so completely absorbed in the show. Taylor Swift delivered such an incredible performance—it didn't matter if you were a superfan, a dad there with your daughter, or a husband tagging along with your wife. Everyone was just into it.

There were people crying around me, there were flames, lights, audience interaction—it was unreal. We left completely blown away. I think the whole country was. And that made me think: *How do we provide that same level of experience—not just to our clients, but also to our team, our agents, and everyone connected to our organization?* Once you can pinpoint what creates that kind of emotional, memorable experience, you can deliver something truly remarkable for both clients and employees.

Another great example is Chick-fil-A. Every time you go, the experience is phenomenal. You pull into a drive-thru with 30 or 40 cars ahead of you, yet you're in and out in just a couple of minutes. The process is so efficient, and you've got three people helping you before you even get to the window. That's what keeps people coming back—*the experience.*

At our agency, we work to create a similar level of excellence for our clients. We have a few key guidelines that we follow. First, we have a rule for customer communication. A lot of agents will say, "I've got to deal with my customer—they need to talk to me." But that's not true. In our agency, we follow the twenty-four-hour rule: No customer goes more than twenty-four hours without a response. That doesn't mean weekends—but within regular business hours, Monday through Friday, every client should receive a response within 24 hours. Our administrative staff is responsible for upholding that rule, and when it's followed, it lays the foundation for exceptional customer service and an outstanding client experience.

Again, think back to Chick-fil-A. What they've done is map out the entire client journey—from the moment someone enters the drive-thru to the moment they drive away. That's what we aim to create within our agency: a mapped-out client experience. When someone calls in, how is that call handled? Who receives it? How is it routed? For us, we send it directly to the administrative staff. Once a client reaches out, our team logs the interaction as an activity in our system. We track that activity until it's closed out—

always adhering to the twenty-four hour rule. Everyone in the agency has a role in the client experience, and that role must be clearly defined.

Let's talk about building long-term relationships. I think back to when I first started visiting clients in person. To this day, I still receive birthday cards and Christmas gifts. One client, Carol, in Decatur, Illinois, gives me a Christmas ornament every year with my kids' names or photos on it. I've received blankets, keepsakes—little things that come from building genuine relationships over time. It all comes down to this: people don't really respond until they know how much you care. You have to show that you truly care about them.

That means taking time to get to know your clients on a personal level. I've always added clients on Facebook, followed their lives, taken notes about their families, milestones, or interests—and I make sure to reference those details during calls. Not as a sales tactic, but because in this industry, if you want to succeed and be a person of influence, you genuinely have to care about people. And they have to feel it and see it. If you don't have the willingness—or the ability—to genuinely care about people and show that consistently, you're setting yourself up for failure. True success is built on authentic, long-term relationships with both your team and your clients.

Five-Star Reviews

Every client receives an automated prompt with the option to leave a review. This is incredibly important—not only for building credibility and attracting new clients, but also for understanding what your current clients think of your service. It's an opportunity to get feedback: what you're doing well, and where you need to improve.

Here's a funny story. We have one four-star review—and it came from an extended family member! The review itself was glowing, but they still gave us four stars. Sometimes, even when you think everything went perfectly, people may still rate you at 80%. That's why it's important to follow up. Reach out and find out what could have made it a five-star experience. We also had a one-star review once. It turned out to be a simple miscommunication. One phone call later, we cleared it up, and the client updated her review to five stars. That just goes to show how powerful it can be to follow up and listen—really listen—to what your clients are saying. They'll tell you if something's wrong. And if they do, it's on you to make it right.

Now, let's talk about annual reviews and client engagement. This is a big part of our process. We tell our clients that we'll be offering annual reviews—and we follow through. In reality, we often provide semi-annual reviews. These reviews give clients a chance to engage with us, ask questions, get updates, and feel that personal touch that deepens the relationship. This step is critical for retention. Ask yourself: *"Is this a one-time transaction? Am I just a call center? Am I like every other agent who sells a policy and then disappears, treating clients like just another number?"* Or... are you creating something closer to that Taylor Swift experience? Something memorable. Something worth talking about. Something they walk away from thinking, *That was not my normal insurance experience. That was something I'm really excited about. I'm genuinely happy to do business with these people.*

It's like the feeling you get after paying $250 for a concert ticket and thinking, *That was worth every penny.* That's the kind of feeling clients need to walk away with. We also host a variety of events to recognize our clients. Every year, we hold a customer appreciation event. Even if clients don't attend, the important part is that the invitation goes out to thousands of them. Maybe only twenty, thirty, or forty people actually show up, but everyone receives the card. And we get emails and texts all the time—*"Hey, thanks for the invite. Can't make it this year."* And that's fine. The point is that clients just want to know they're appreciated. They want to feel like there's an event for *them*—not a sales event, not something to generate revenue, but something that simply shows gratitude. They want to feel appreciated, valued, and respected. Everyone wants that. When you host an event to support your community—whether through volunteer work, offering a service, or simply showing you care—it goes a long way not just with your existing clients, but with the larger community around you as well.

For our agents, we take the same approach. We provide personalized onboarding and do a lot of goal setting within our team. That kind of intentional effort is just as important internally as it is externally. You've got to provide that same experience for your team. I mentioned earlier that we recently hosted a private event in Nashville, Tennessee. It was entirely focused on celebrating our team. We created a once-in-a-lifetime experience—and it worked. Weeks later, people are still talking about it. Honestly, Emily and I are still talking about it. It was incredible.

We're fortunate to be surrounded by amazing people, and because of that, we get to be part of some really special things. When you take a moment to reflect on the best moments in your life, it's not the cars or houses that come to mind—it's the experiences. For me, I think back to when my child was born, and I was part of the delivery. That's something I'll never forget. It can never be taken away. It was an incredible experience. I also think of our family vacations to Watercolor, Florida. That's the one place where I feel truly removed from work and business. Those trips are priceless. If you can create those kinds of unforgettable experiences within your company—like we've done with our annual summits or special events—you set a cultural standard that's hard to match.

We also offer a lot of private coaching and training. That's really what the COACHG platform is all about. One of my favorite events is in Destin, Florida. It's a private gathering for COACHG members held at a 13,000-square-foot mansion. Sure, we do some coaching and talking—but most of it is about the experience. It's about connection, networking, and creating something memorable. We have hibachi come in, we host shrimp boils, we go to the beach—we do all kinds of fun things. And those are memories that will stick with me forever. They can't be taken away. I think that's something our partners really value as well—or at least, I hope they do more than anything.

And when I do private coaching—when I do a one-on-one—that's a paid session, first and foremost. And again, it's like a ticket to a Taylor Swift concert. If someone is exchanging money for my time, it has to be an incredible experience. One where they walk away saying, *I would've paid triple. I would've paid four or five times that for the value and the experience I got.* Creating that kind of experience is all about truly understanding who you're working with, building relationships, and ensuring that their time with you lasts far beyond the sale or any monetary exchange.

EMILY

I want to approach this topic from a different angle—by going back to the root of everything: your company culture, your vision, your mission, and your values. It all begins with focusing on the employee experience. Throughout my career, I've focused deeply on a concept called the Service Profit Chain, a theory developed by researchers at Harvard University. The concept states that if you take care of your employees, they'll take care of your guests. And naturally, from those great guest experiences, you'll see profitability. So when I think about the client experience, so much of it depends on how engaged your employees are—how "bought-in" they are to the mission, the vision, and the culture you're creating, as well as the service you're delivering. When you invest in your team, you're able to drive forward together toward your shared goals. It makes the entire process more enjoyable, more meaningful, and more exciting.

A big part of that culture also involves defining what a five-star client experience looks like. What does it look like from an agent's perspective? From an admin's perspective? You need to be very clear during onboarding and training about what's expected and why it matters. The other day, I was answering the phone because our admin was out, and Chase looked at me and said, "Does everybody answer the phone like that?" And I said, "Yeah." That's part of it—being consistent in what you're trying to deliver. When you think about the customer experience, it's bigger than just the client. It's about how you take care of your employees. How do you engage them? How do you inspire them to care for your clients, customers, or consumers—whatever that may look like in your business? When they enjoy what they do, they'll naturally go the extra mile. And when that happens, I believe you'll see profitability and success come back tenfold.

EIGHT
KEEP SCORE LIKE A PRO

As we move through building an agency, building a team, and really getting things rocking and rolling, financial mastery becomes a really important topic. I think this is where a lot of people—especially business and insurance agency owners—tend to run into issues. In my opinion, that's because many people in the insurance industry aren't true business owners. Insurance has a very low barrier to entry, and in many ways, it's fairly easy to scale a team. That said, business acumen doesn't always come along with team building.

From my own experience over the past 10 years—learning from mistakes, mishaps, and, for lack of a better word, failures—I've come to believe that mastering this area early on can be hugely beneficial in the long run. I think back to my earlier years when I was pretty good with personal finances. I didn't have to worry much about financial mastery, and I didn't have a lot of overhead. One of the great things about insurance is that you *can* scale with minimal overhead. For me, early on, overhead wasn't much of a concern. Because of that, things like tracking financials, KPIs, and budgeting were on the back burner.

Once we began developing our team and scaling aggressively, financial mastery was forced to the forefront. Suddenly, we were looking at some pretty major marketing expenses. Right now, we spend over $100,000 a month on advertising alone—not counting our other marketing sources. At that point, it became absolutely critical to track metrics, prepare for the future, allocate funds appropriately, and start thinking like a big company. That meant budgeting by category, forecasting profits and losses, and establishing sound financial practices.

One of the key topics I want to highlight in this financial mastery chapter is setting clear roles and responsibilities. For example, we have a commissions department. In my opinion, that alone is a full-time job. You need someone fully responsible for tracking commissions and capturing discrepancies. We get paid by thirty to forty different companies every week or month, and it's crucial to have someone consolidating those payments, ensuring accurate tracking, and making sure your team is being paid correctly—so your business isn't underpaying or overpaying anyone. If you want to scale, I think the commissions department is one of the most important roles to establish early on—especially in a commission-driven industry like insurance. Get someone in that role who can grow with you. There are also some third-party services I would recommend researching and vetting early on.

Another huge area is budgeting and financial planning. I believe every business should sit down each year and map out a twelve-month budget—what you plan to spend or expect to spend across various categories. For us, major expense areas include multiple office buildings we own (rent and lease), as well as advertising and marketing. You also need to understand your payroll and forecast future needs—whether that's additional capital for hiring or reinvestment in the business to support growth. These are big categories. And while I won't go too deep into budgeting and financial planning here, if you're serious about growing and scaling, this is something you should focus on. It's essential to build a proper budget and financial plan. That's also a key focus during our Game Plan sessions: helping agency owners work on their business, not just in it. That's where the real progress happens.

KPIs and Production Trackers

KPI stands for Key Performance Indicator. These are the metrics that tell the story—whether or not you're performing the way you should be within your agency. For us, some of the most important KPIs include first-year commissions. Are we hitting that $1,000 to $1,200 to $1,500 range in first-year commission per client? In other words, are you maximizing revenue per client?

Another major KPI is return on ad spend. In my opinion, those are the two most critical metrics we need to monitor to determine if we're doing well. If I have those two numbers, I can tell whether we're performing or not. I know a lot of other people use different KPIs, but for us, those are the primary ones we track to evaluate performance.

Monthly Reporting

We're constantly reviewing our monthly P&Ls and looking at year-over-year data. Where are we spending? Are we overspending in certain areas? Underspending? Are we over budget or under budget? Where can we improve our internal processes and systems? For me, hiring for this role has been a game-changer.

Our director of business development now provides these reports, identifies trends or issues in advance, and then we work through them together. Having someone else manage and present this information has been incredibly valuable.

Maximizing Profitability

This brings us to what I call *intentional congruency*. Many people don't realize how many different ways a business can generate income—ways that all feed the core engine. I often draw a circle and put "Revenue Generation" in the center. Around it, I ask: how many different things in your agency can generate revenue? For us, it's a lot:

- External partners
- Internal production
- COACHG revenue
- Sponsorship revenue
- Event revenue
- Office/Space Rental

There are so many avenues that contribute to profitability. The key is identifying which revenue streams *congruently* fit within your business and can add value without distraction. One example is annuities. A lot of people in our industry don't offer retirement planning. I call this an invisible revenue stream. We don't spend a single extra penny in marketing costs for this revenue—we simply uncover it from our current clients and add roughly 30% to our top line.

Another example is supplemental health products (ancillary). Most agents don't cross-sell ancillary products or explore other lines of insurance or specialties. By offering products like cancer, heart/stroke, hospital indemnity, home care, recovery care, life, and accident policies, we again add another 30% to our top line. But those are additional areas that can feed the beast, as I like to say. Ask yourself: *"Am I maximizing your revenue streams?"*

Sheehan's Wall

We discussed Sheehan's Wall earlier in the book: There's a large brick wall in front of you. You've got a sledgehammer, and your goal is to break through it. Now, if you swing that sledgehammer and hit twenty different spots randomly, you won't make much progress. But if you hit the same spot over and over again, you'll eventually break through. That's what success looks like in the insurance industry. You focus on one revenue stream. You pound that same spot over and over again until you've built mastery. Then, you diversify.

That's exactly how we built our agency. We started with a singular focus: turning 65 leads. And once we built that into something strong, we began to diversify into other areas. We brought in annuity revenue. We brought in ancillary revenue. And pretty soon, we were teaching others how to do the same—that's how COACHG was created. So get really good at that *one* thing, and then, guess what? You can teach it. Then, you can diversify. Sheehan's Wall is a concept that I believe is crucial to mastering financial strategy. If you want to increase your revenue tenfold, focus deeply on one area—master it—and *then* diversify.

Reinvestment

Reinvestment is another key aspect of financial mastery. Ask yourself: *"Am I reinvesting profit back into the business each year? Feeding my business to keep it healthy?"* Think about how we treat our bodies—when we fuel them with nutritious foods, they perform at their best. The same principle applies to your business. When you invest in it intentionally, it runs like a high-performing vehicle. We've reinvested in multiple ways:

- **Office Buildings:** We have several office buildings—sometimes I think we might even have too many! But they serve a purpose. They give our team a central space to work and collaborate. They allow affiliate partners to come in for training, provide a venue for consumer seminars, and help attract new partners and internal team members.
- **Branding Campaigns:** We invest heavily in branding—billboards, TV campaigns, and more. These initiatives don't always yield immediate returns, but they set us apart in a crowded market over the long term.
- **People:** This is, by far, our most important investment. Just a couple of months ago, we spent between $75,000 and $100,000 on our team over a two-day experience—including bonuses and intentional appreciation. Reinvesting in your people is the most impactful thing you can do.

At its core, **reinvestment** is about spending money to make more. You put one dollar in, and you should be getting two dollars or more out. That's the mindset.

Systems

Another major area of reinvestment is systems. Yes, there are upfront costs, but if done right, systems save you time and money —and they should provide a strong return on investment over time. For us, one of the biggest reinvestments is in The Coach's Office. We now have hundreds of agents from across the country who choose to reinvest in themselves by joining this community. It's a space where agents can learn, grow, develop, and connect with like-minded peers. Over the years, I've realized that the best reinvestment is in people—specifically, surrounding yourself with the right people. I can't say this enough: if you're around three or four people who are doing something bigger and better than you are, before long, you'll become the fifth. That's exactly what The Coach's Office provides.

EMILY

My perspective on this topic comes more from the cultural side of things. To me, financial mastery is a journey—it's something you continue to learn, something you commit to improving. That means surrounding yourself with the right people, the right mentors, and the right tools to help you dig deeper into this area. It may be something that comes naturally to you, or it might be a little uncomfortable. Either way, the important thing is to know where you stand on that spectrum and find support accordingly. When you do that—when you approach it with the right mindset—you'll be equipped to identify and act on the things that truly move the needle in your business.

The second thing I think a lot about when it comes to this topic is how important it is to communicate, teach, and mentor your employees. Anyone who's along for the ride with you should have a strong understanding of how the business functions, what drives it forward, and how they, as employees, contribute to that success. We've talked a lot about this in the second half of the book. One example is ensuring that your team knows what your key performance indicators (KPIs) are—and how the business is performing against them. Because let's face it: everyone performs better when you're keeping score! Sharing that insight helps your team feel more invested in the success of your organization.

That said, I think it's a delicate balance. Going back to the concept I mentioned earlier—The Service Profit Chain—you'll remember the idea that when you fully engage your people, they'll naturally take care of your clients. That, in turn, elevates the customer experience and leads to greater profitability. It's important to keep the conversation rooted in your company's vision and mission, while still communicating the financial piece. You want to strike the right balance—you don't want to lean too heavily in either direction. If you focus too much on finances, your purpose-driven employees might feel disconnected or uninspired. On the other hand, if you avoid the numbers, your more data-driven team members may find the messaging vague or ungrounded.

That's why understanding your team—and delivering the right balance of purpose and performance metrics—is key. Once you start to grasp the metrics yourself, your next step is to help your team understand them, and to communicate in a way that resonates. When you do that, you're going to see the results you're looking for—even faster.

NINE
SCALE THE ROSTER

I love this chapter on scaling an agency and the topic of scaling in general. There are some key components you need to be aware of, think through, and even write down.

The first one is: What is the end goal? Are you building your agency for a big acquisition? Are you looking to leave a legacy? Do you want to pass it down to your family? Or are you aiming to make it employee-owned? What's your purpose—and why are you doing it? For us, I think back to when I was coaching. That experience shaped a lot of how I approach business today. When you boil it down, coaching filled a void—and legacy became a huge part of our mission. We want to leave something that lasts well beyond us—not just for our family, but for our employees' families, and for generations after them. Back when I was coaching, what I loved most was being part of a team—leading a team, being in the locker room, sharing camaraderie, winning together, and even losing together. Having people you can lean on.

The insurance business can be lonely—especially as a solo agent. It's a lot of phone calls. A lot of no's. A lot of time alone.

Bringing people onto the team changed that. It made insurance fun again. It made it exciting. It felt like sports. And when you think about it—business *is* a sport. There's nothing like winning. And there's *definitely* nothing like winning with a group of people you love being around and celebrating with. That's been huge for us.

On the legacy side, impact has always mattered deeply to Emily and me. How do we leave a legacy that's bigger than us—bigger than our family—and truly influences our communities? We realized that alone, we could only go so far. But with a team, we could go *so much farther*. That realization was a major part of our decision to scale. Just a few weeks ago, we rolled out our vision to grow the company to a $100 million valuation within the next three to five years. We communicated that to our team in a *big* way. What we saw in response was alignment, excitement—and people realizing they now have the opportunity to change *their* family's future. That meant everything to us.

For us, it all comes down to two things: legacy, and being part of a winning team that shares the wins—and the losses—together. But for you, you've got to define what's important to *you*. You need to get clear on the what and the why behind your agency. Because if you don't know those two things, you're going to struggle to scale in a sustainable way.

I also believe that duplicating what works is a huge part of scaling. I spent years trying to figure it all out on my own. But finding the whos—the people who had already figured out the how—made all the difference. They say not to reinvent the wheel, and I think that advice applies perfectly to growing an insurance agency. There are proven formulas out there—and there are a lot of unproven ones. The key is finding the right systems, the right partnerships, and the right *whos* can help you replicate what already works. And then, ultimately, you've got to duplicate yourself.

I say it time and time again—and it's one of the most important things you'll ever do if you want to scale. I spent years being a top producer. I've got more awards in boxes than you can count. But you can only do so much as an individual. Literally—you can only go so far on your own. Once you realize that, scaling becomes all about duplicating yourself. You might be the best producer in the world, but if you can teach someone to do 75% of what you do, that's a win. Now teach five people to do 75% of what you do—and pretty soon, your agency is humming. You're producing 300% to 400% more than you ever could alone. That's the path to real scale: duplicating yourself, and then empowering those people to duplicate themselves. It can be a really fun and rewarding process —especially if you have the heart of a teacher or a coach. I believe that if that's you, scaling is inevitable.

Optimizing Systems

This is a big one. We're constantly working to improve our systems and processes. That's how you scale efficiently, especially on the tech side—by putting the right systems in place and letting automation do its job, giving you back time and freedom. Right now, we're exploring outsourcing our commissions department to a third-party vendor for $2,500 a month. Currently, we pay our internal commissions liaison over $45,000 a year. At first glance, $25,000 annually for outsourcing might seem steep—but if it saves time and streamlines the process, it can free up our team to focus on what they do best. That's what optimized systems should do: save time, increase productivity, and put people in positions to win.

Strategic Partnerships

Strategic partnership is one of my favorite topics—and something I talk about often in our Coach's Office community. Collaboration leads to innovation. Finding the right people to partner with can be a game-changer. For example, I met Joe Pate in April 2024 at one of our annual events in Destin, Florida—our Destin Mastermind. I invited him to speak, and within two months, we were doing business together. Now, Joe is one of my best friends. He's a huge part of The Coach's Office, and I'm incredibly proud of our partnership and friendship. I truly believe we elevate each other. There are plenty of other partnerships I could highlight in this book that have done the same. The point is: *Who are the people out there with whom you can create mutually beneficial partnerships? The ones who can help launch your business—and vice versa?* That's where the magic happens: when you find aligned partners and build something great together.

Brand Awareness

Emily will speak to this more, but let me say—your brand is about so much more than a logo or a color scheme. It's how people feel about you. It's what they think when they hear your name. For us, our brand goes far beyond paper or design—it's the experience we provide. It's what people associate us with. We're seeing the COACHG platform and The Coach's Office take off, because people associate our brand with excellence. They believe that when they come in, their agency will skyrocket. That belief is based on results—but it's also rooted in what our brand represents. Our brand says: We create championship producers. We build championship teams. And we execute on that promise. That's the power of brand awareness.

When done right, your brand tells your story—before you ever say a word. You need to be able to tell your story through your brand—and people need to know that story. We've built a lot of frequency into our branding. We post daily across our consumer brands. We've got billboards, TV ads, and more. People are constantly aware of what we do—and they need to be. The same goes for you. If people don't know what you do, how can they work with you? I'm not a big Grant Cardone guy, but there's one thing he says that always sticks with me: "If they don't know you, they can't flow you." That's 100% true. People have to know you. They have to be aware of you. Awareness leads to opportunity—and opportunity leads to growth.

Brand awareness matters. Focus on what you do best. That's really been the key to our growth over the past few years. As Emily always says: "Focus on your strengths and hire your weaknesses." And after 10 years, I've finally embraced that fully. We've identified what I do best—relationships, communication, recruiting, and high-level sales strategy. It makes sense because when I was coaching, that's what I was doing every day: building relationships with players, recruiting students from across the country to invest in a private school education. What I'm doing now isn't that different—just a different setting, a different product. But the heart of it is still connection and vision.

On the flip side, we need to be aware of something I call opportunity confusion. I talk about this often, especially with new agency owners. When people come to me with a hundred ideas, the first thing I tell them to do is make a list—rank their top ten opportunities. Then we pick one thing to focus on. Just one. And honestly, I'm speaking to myself here too. As entrepreneurs, business owners, and agency leaders, we constantly have things flying at us. Ideas. Opportunities. Distractions. The best business owners learn how to identify the biggest opportunities—and execute on them. If I were you, I'd make that list, focus on the top one, and go do it.

Intentional Congruency

You've heard me talk about intentional congruency throughout the book—doing things that align with and support the mission of your business. Things that "touch the line." Chuck McDowell talked about this when I had the pleasure of interviewing him on the COACHG podcast. "Touching the line" can mean a few things. In sports, it's about going all the way. No shortcuts. Working until the towel is soaked. Finishing with the details.

In business, "touching the line" means that everything you do either helps or hurts your business. There is no neutral. Every action either moves you forward—or holds you back. Every decision, every investment, every conversation should touch the line of positively impacting your company. So focus on that. Stay aligned. If you can apply the ideas in this chapter—brand awareness, focus, intentional congruency—you'll be well on your way to scaling your agency in a way that's sustainable, effective, and efficient.

EMILY

Scaling an agency is the big leagues, right? This is where everything we've talked about starts to come together. Whether you're transitioning from a solo agency to adding your first employee, or you're building out a full team, scaling means doing something *bigger*. I want to go back to something we talked about earlier—culture. Laying that cultural foundation from the beginning will serve you tremendously on your scaling journey.

Defining who you are and what you believe in is critical. It helps guide your decisions as you grow. As Chase mentioned, scaling brings a lot of opportunity—new relationships, new ventures—but it also comes with tough decisions. You'll need to be sure you're doing what's right for you, your employees, your brand, and your business. The goal is to scale in a way that feels aligned—where you're confident, comfortable, and proud of the path you're taking. Sure, you might come across opportunities that generate a lot of cash flow quickly—but are they sustainable? Do they reflect your brand promise?

Even recently, as COACHG has continued to grow, we've had some major internal discussions about opportunities that came our way. The questions we ask are always the same: Does this align with what we're trying to accomplish? Does this align with the COACHG brand? Sometimes the answer is *yes* in one area but *no* in another. That's why it's so important to know your boundaries. And while those may evolve over time—as your culture naturally evolves with growth—you need a North Star. Something to come back to consistently. It will guide you through the noise. Also, don't forget to bring your employees along with you. Share what you're doing and why. Help them understand what you're trying to accomplish. That alignment will only help you move faster and more effectively.

TEN
MAKE THE ADJUSTMENTS

As we near the end of this book, I wanted to dedicate a chapter to something that's been critical over the last decade of my career: innovation and adaptation. Looking back, I can confidently say that being able to innovate and adapt has been one of the *key* components of growing and scaling our agency. You have to be ready for change—whether it's new industry trends, shifts in the market, or emerging tools like AI. There's so much happening so fast, and your ability to adapt will determine how far you go.

One thing we always do is look at our 12-month goals, but we also plan three to five years out. We're not just reacting to the present—we're forecasting the future. Recently, we rolled out our new three-to-five-year plan to the team. It was an exciting moment. We laid out the vision, shared the blueprint, and gave them a clear picture of what we're working toward. That kind of long-term planning allows you to start building the infrastructure you'll need for what's ahead.

For example, right now we have 16 internal employees. But to get to our goal—a $100 million valuation in five years—we know we'll need significantly more team members, stronger systems, and intentional growth across every department. Forecasting lets us reverse-engineer that future and build toward it now. We're going to need to double—almost triple—our staff. So we have to start building out that infrastructure now. And that means, of course, expanding our office space. Currently, we're renovating the top floor of one of our office buildings to accommodate twelve to fifteen new employees over the next twelve to eighteen months. Being able to see that future clearly allows us to prepare for it and adapt effectively.

On the innovation side, it's about more than just systems—it's about fostering a culture that creates and empowers leaders to be innovative and then letting them do their thing. Having a strong leadership team and an incredible culture has been one of the most important drivers of innovation in our company. Just today, we met as a leadership team and gave each department the chance to share what they're working on, what ideas they have, and how they're improving their areas of the business. Letting our people take ownership, be creative, and bring forward their ideas has been critical to our growth. Innovation and adaptation start with the right people—and giving them the space and support to lead.

Intentional congruency comes into play here as well. When we talk about innovation, one thing we've done really well is ensuring that every new initiative feeds the main engine of the business—revenue. COACHG is a perfect example of that. At the end of the day, COACHG supports everything we do. It brings in new agents, forms strategic partnerships, creates event opportunities, fosters collaborations—and generates revenue. It's an innovative platform that also aligns with our core business goals. That's intentional congruency. As you think about your own agency, ask yourself: *"What can I create that supports what I already do well? What can I innovate internally that aligns with our mission and opens new doors?"*

Forecasting is another key component. What does your industry look like three years from now? How do you prepare for that today? Take industry trends—those are critical. I think back to 2020 during COVID. You either adapted, or you went out of business. There was no middle ground. At the time, we were a "boots-on-the-ground" company. Most of our business was done face-to-face. But we made the decision to adapt, and we shifted almost completely to a virtual model. Now, 80% of our business is virtual, and only 20% is in person. That shift was a direct result of adaptation—keeping up with where we saw the industry headed: toward a more digital, remote experience. The lesson? Things are always changing. You have to be willing—and ready—to change with them. While no one can predict a global event like COVID, you can forecast where your industry is headed. You can prepare. And that's the key to long-term success.

Professional development is a huge part of that preparation. The Coach's Office is one of the industry's leading resources for professional growth. It helps you connect with other agents, optimize your systems, improve your structure, and learn from like-minded people committed to growth. But beyond our platform, there are always events, conferences, and tools in your industry. One area I think is especially important for development is technology. Staying ahead on the tech side can give you a massive advantage—and make your business more scalable, efficient, and future-ready. One thing we really strive to do is develop our team —and especially our leaders—on the technology side, while also helping them grow professionally as leaders.

That brings me to something I think we all need to reflect on regularly: Who's coaching you? It's a question I ask myself all the time: How am I developing professionally? I'm fortunate to lead and coach hundreds of insurance agents and agencies across the country—but at the end of the day, I still need coaching too. As leaders—whether you're an agency owner, executive, or department head—it's essential to keep growing. And it's just as important to invest in the development of your leadership team. There are so many opportunities for growth within the industry: events, mentors, coaching programs, new systems, and tools. Identifying and acting on those opportunities is key.

One quote I always come back to is from Coach Burt. In his Greatness Factory, there's a sign that says: "Money changes hands when problems are solved." Think about that. It couldn't be more true. When we talk about innovation and adaptation, it all comes down to solving problems. If you solve big problems, you earn big returns. And that's something we have to keep front and center as business owners. If you're not solving a problem, there's no real reason for someone to buy from you, switch to your service, or work with you. So ask yourself: *"What problems are we solving?"* And remember—the bigger the problem, the bigger the money.

Collaboration leads to innovation. The biggest leaps—whether in our company, our business, or even our personal lives—have always come from people. From collaboration. So I encourage you: build those relationships. Collaborate. You never know which connection or conversation will lead to your next quantum leap.

EMILY

When I think about innovation, I think about how important it is to weave it into your culture from the very beginning. We live in a world where things are changing constantly—and quickly. If you're not paying attention to trends in your industry, if you're not embracing innovation and adapting, you're going to face serious challenges when it comes to success, and especially to scaling and growing. One of the most powerful things you can do is bring your team along for the ride. When your team understands that innovation is part of your culture—that adapting is not just allowed, but *expected*—you'll be able to mitigate a lot of the fear that often comes with change.

Fear of change is real. I've been part of well-established, long-standing brands where that fear sounded like: "Well, we've always done it this way." That mindset can hold companies back. But if you set clear expectations from day one—that change is part of the process, that innovation is embedded in how you do business—it becomes easier for your team to embrace it. That's how you build a culture that's resilient, responsive, and ready for whatever comes next.

Another important consideration is identifying who the innovators are in your business—who naturally thinks innovatively, who's passionate about looking ahead, and who's always thinking about the future of your industry or the way your business operates. Understanding the strengths of your team members and leadership team will help you move forward effectively. It ensures people are in the right roles, doing the right things. I'll be the first to admit—innovation isn't necessarily my personal strength. But I am really good at asking the right questions, identifying gaps, and integrating the ideas that are being considered. And I'm self-aware enough to recognize that. That's actually where Chase and I make a great team. He's incredibly innovative in the way he thinks, and I bring a complementary skill set that helps us collaborate and ultimately arrive at a strong, well-rounded, finished product.

So when you're thinking about innovation—especially when you're about to make a big leap—it's crucial to have the right skills in the room. You want different perspectives that can challenge ideas, poke holes, and then help integrate and execute them. That kind of collaboration is what leads not only to great ideas—but to actual execution. And that's what gets you to the finish line.

ELEVEN
LEAVE A LEGACY

Legacy and succession planning is an incredibly hot topic in the insurance industry right now. Over the past few years, we've seen major private equity firms acquiring some of the biggest names in the business. It's become the "cool" thing to do—to be acquired or to say you're building a business designed to be acquired. But I don't think a lot of people truly understand what that means, what the implications are, or even if that's really the route they want to take. That's what this chapter is about: diving into those questions and helping you identify what your true end goal is. That's where succession planning starts—what is your end goal? Or as Taylor Swift would say, what's your end game? Understanding that is going to help you decide which legacy or succession planning path is right for you.

Let me start by saying this: the most important part of succession planning is developing the leaders within your company. Looking back over the past few years, we've had some phenomenal producers in our organization. And I made the mistake of assuming that great producers would automatically make great leaders. That's not always the case. In fact, it's often not the case. Just like in sports, not all great players make great coaches. I've seen it time and time again—top performers who simply aren't built to lead others. So when you move someone into a leadership position, they need to be developed. That's the phase of business we're in right now—really shaping our company into a legacy model and putting long-term succession plans in place. That starts with leadership development.

If we can raise up leaders who can run the company, then Emily and I will be in a position to enjoy what we've built—and manage from a distance. Developing leaders means coaching the coaches. That's where we spend a lot of our time. We have direct reports, and it's my job to develop *them*—to make sure they're equipped to lead *their* teams and oversee *their* departments with excellence. Leadership development is one of the most important—and most overlooked—parts of succession planning. If you want to build a company that's worth acquiring, worth selling, worth passing on... it all comes down to developing your people.

Now, let's talk about exit strategies—because there are a few common types, and it's important to understand the differences. One type is a full exit. This is where you completely step away from the business—you sell it outright, and you're done. You ride off into the sunset, so to speak. Surprisingly, that type of exit isn't always the most lucrative. Why? Because if the buyer has to take over the company without you, they're assuming all the risk. They now have to run and manage the business entirely on their own, which typically results in a lower valuation compared to other exit structures. So while it may sound like the ideal scenario, a full exit often lands in the mid-tier range in terms of financial return.

Typically, in our industry right now, you can expect around a 2x to 3x valuation if you're completely exiting the business. When I say two to three times, I'm referring to your earnings before interest, taxes, depreciation, and amortization (EBITDA). So, for those looking to fully exit, that's the ballpark: you find a buyer, they acquire the company, you step away entirely, hand over all assets and revenue, and either retire or move on to a different business venture.

Another popular model is an acquisition with continued involvement, where a buyer (often private equity) acquires your company but expects you to keep running it. This is probably the most common model in our industry today. In this case, they're not just buying your business—they're buying the machine. They want the systems, the structure, the revenue—but they also want you to stay involved and continue growing the business. In these situations, the valuation multiple is typically much higher. A reasonable range in this model is 7x to 11x EBITDA, depending on the size, growth, and profitability of your company. Some deals have seen higher than 11x.

But keep in mind—you're now working for someone else. You've sold all or the majority of the business, but you're still running it. You're essentially an employee of what used to be your company. Yes, you get a nice check and liquidity, but many people misunderstand this type of succession plan. You're still responsible for growth, and now there are a lot more voices at the table—more oversight, more decision-makers, and more expectations.

One model we've recently implemented—and something I'm really excited about—is the managing partner model. We restructured our company into 100 million shares and began distributing equity to key employees. We used phantom stock, which I encourage you to research if you want more detail. The point is, we believed it was critical—especially as we rolled out our 3-to-5-year plan and long-term succession strategy—that our employees were truly part of it. Whether we eventually pursue a full exit or an acquisition, we want the people who helped us build this company to benefit from it. They deserve a piece of what they've helped create. I highly recommend this approach to anyone who's building something special. If you want your team to be fully invested in your mission and your long-term vision, they need skin in the game. That was incredibly important to us. Our team now has opportunities to earn more equity, and I believe that's one of the best ways to build something truly meaningful and lasting. When your people feel that sense of ownership—not just symbolically, but financially—they're more committed, more aligned, and more excited about the future. So, we've done the managing partner model, and I'm really excited as we continue growing with it. I think it's going to pay massive dividends down the road.

Another area I want to touch on is mergers and acquisitions. When I talk about mergers, I mean the kind that typically happens as part of preparing for an acquisition—as a way to strengthen your position. I've seen different examples where lead companies merge with insurance companies to bulk up, or where two insurance companies join forces. It's a strategic way to bring two assets together, and in many cases, I would recommend this approach. Usually, a successful merger involves two complementary partners that bring value to each other. I wouldn't want to merge with a business that's identical to mine—it doesn't add any external value. Instead, I'd want to merge with a company that brings in additional resources and helps us enhance what we're already doing. I think that's when a merger really makes sense.

From there, you can also pursue acquisitions. A couple of years ago, I acquired a small insurance company, and we're currently in the middle of acquiring another one. These are full acquisitions—those agency owners are exiting the business to retire or move on to other things. You can acquire different insurance agencies, aim for that two to three times multiple, bring on their clients, service them well, and ultimately grow your revenue and bottom line through acquisition.

It's important to understand how you want to grow your business. Some people want to leave it to their children and keep it in the family for generations. So, get really clear on what's important to you and what your end game is. Understanding that early on can help prevent issues later down the road.

EMILY

Legacy and succession planning is definitely a passion of mine—something I've learned a lot about and had the opportunity to engage in throughout my career. The truth is, legacy isn't just about who takes over—it's about what endures after you've stepped out of the room. It's about what you leave behind. We've all seen organizations change leadership at the top and then lose their way because the incoming leader had a drastically different focus than their predecessor. That's where succession planning becomes crucial—and where taking a holistic approach really matters.

I remember sitting in meetings over the years, discussing the strengths of individuals in various departments and the skills and experience they'd need to reach the next level. Development played a critical role in determining whether someone was prepared for that next step. Often, it took a year or two of focused preparation to get them there. A big part of that preparation also involved understanding where the organization was heading and what types of roles would be necessary to get it there. The key is to prepare individuals for growth long before the company is actually ready for the role—especially at the leadership level, but really across all layers of the business.

Another important component to keep in mind is taking a

holistic view of all the qualities you're developing—not just the skills required for a specific role. You also want to be evaluating their leadership abilities. How do they engage with employees? How do they embody the company culture, contribute to it, and help sustain it? Considering how continuity will be maintained in all these areas is crucial to preserving the very things you've worked hard to build. Make sure you are actively involved in the succession planning process. That may include creating and/or participating in individual development plans for each person you're looking to grow—and ensuring that those plans remain a strong priority for everyone involved.

This might mean touching on an element of the plan in each one-on-one meeting with your employee, followed by a full quarterly review to assess progress. It's about putting a process in place to ensure consistent development. Ultimately, it comes down to taking time to work *on* the business, not just *in* it. It's about defining roles, clearly communicating, and doing all the foundational work that will prepare you—whatever your end game may be.

TWELVE
THE PLAYS I'D CALL DIFFERENTLY

This is probably my favorite chapter. And as you'll see from the things I wish I had done differently as a solo agent, there are a lot of similarities to the things I wish I had done differently as an agency—as a company. The first thing I would have done? Get married sooner. All jokes aside, I think the biggest thing that really launched our agency was bringing in Emily. As you've seen throughout this book, she brings a whole different perspective—a whole new way of looking at things—that was really missing in our company.

That helped us build a "We Company." Looking back, what I truly wish I had done differently was to build a *We* Company instead of a *Me* Company. I used to think, especially when I had a small team, that we were already a We Company. I thought we were unified, that we were a team, and that I was doing everything I could for them—but I was far from that. It was really just a bunch of "me" people running around. What we've done over the last couple of years is build this incredible We Company, where everyone supports and benefits from each other.

It's truly a family. And I don't use that word lightly in business. These are people I trust with my family, with my children—people I actually want to be around even when I'm not working. I think that's the end game, right? To wake up excited to go to work, to make a difference, and to have an impact every single day. And I truly feel I have that now. I get to go to work every day, and I'm so excited to be around our team—to lead them and develop them. It's something I don't take for granted. But that all happened because we made a conscious decision to become a We Company rather than a Me Company. So if you're looking to build a team, I urge you to think in terms of us rather than me, and I believe you'll be on the right track.

Reinvesting in people and systems is a bit redundant from the first chapter, but it's just so important. As Emily always says, your people are your product. You have to reinvest in them like crazy. When I think back to the most memorable moments in our company, it's always the trips we've taken with carrier partners, or the annual summits we hold in Nashville with our internal team. Those things cost a lot, but our team loves them. They cherish those moments. Reinvesting in our internal team—whether it's raises, bonuses, or anything else we can do to enhance their lives—has been a real blessing. And when it comes to reinvesting in systems, that's something we've leaned on heavily over the past few years. We do everything we can to make our employees' jobs easier. If it saves them time, we're interested. If it can automate something, we're reinvesting in it. People and systems are absolutely critical to scaling and growing at a serious rate. Honestly, those are the two things I wish I had focused on much sooner than I did.

When it comes to brand and marketing, I used to think, "Okay, I'll just make a few Facebook posts," or "I'll throw a logo together." But there's so much more to it than that. We've developed such a strong brand that we're now recognized as a local leader among consumers—and we're quickly becoming a national leader on the agent side. Agents are looking to us as one of the premier places to grow as a producer, scale their company, and build a team. So, our brand—well, we really sat down and got intentional about it. It's wild to think back to April 2024. Emily and I were in Watercolor, Florida, and we had been talking about COACHG and this bigger vision. We were trying to hone in on what the company was really all about. And we just kept circling back to this sports concept: we want to create championship producers. We want to build championship teams—just like a sports organization. We wanted to develop great players, and then bring them together to form a great team.

Watching that vision come alive over the past twelve months has been incredible. Everyone has bought into the concept. Everyone has embraced the brand and the vision. People love what COACHG represents—and that's the power of a strong brand and a clear message. It's something people feel a part of. It's something tangible. Everyone wants to be part of something fresh, cool, and fun—and that's exactly what branding and marketing can do. They create emotion. They make people *feel* something—just from a logo or a mission statement. That feeling can move mountains. Looking back, I wish we had focused on elevating our brand and sharpening our messaging much earlier. If we had, I think we could have accelerated our growth even more.

Proactive recruiting is another key piece. I remember about five years ago, I tried to start a downline agency. But I didn't have the support, the systems, or the infrastructure in place, and it really didn't work out. Fortunately, over the last five years, a lot of high-quality people have found us—through our branding, our marketing, and our mission. But if I could go back, I would've had a much stronger hiring and recruiting plan from the start. I would have been far more proactive. If you want to grow a company, build a team, or scale something meaningful, you have to take a proactive approach. Even if you're not quite ready to make your first hire, even if you can't yet bring on that first team member—you *still* need to have the vision. You have to see it in your mind before you can make it real. That's crucial. Start planning for it now, and, eventually, you'll be able to bring it to life.

Another big lesson is to eliminate distractions. Stop dabbling and doing so many side hustles, go all in! Earlier in the book, I mentioned how I'd sometimes spend Tuesdays or Thursdays at the pool—because I could, as a solo agency owner. That was the life I thought I wanted. But deep down, what I really wanted was to be part of a team. To *build* something bigger. And those distractions held me back from going after that. If I had eliminated those distractions and plugged into the right communities and opportunities, it could've made a huge difference much earlier. So I encourage you—eliminate the distractions. Get involved with The Coach's Office. It's going to be more than a program—it's a club, a membership, a *community* you can plug into and grow with. And really, staying focused is what will keep you from going off track more than anything.

I also think I should've been bolder from the beginning. My wife would probably laugh hearing me say that—most people already consider me a bold person. But early on, I really wasn't. I think that boldness came *after* success. It's easier to be bold when things are working. Confidence is often the memory of success—and boldness is, too. But to *get* to that point, you have to be bold before the success shows up. You have to take chances. So I encourage you: take some chances. I used to ask myself, "What's the worst that could happen?" I'd end up back on a couch. And honestly, when you don't have a lot going on, the real risk is opportunity risk—what you might miss out on if you play it too safe. So again, be bold. Take the leap.

One last thing is—something I've said many times—to partner strategically, and to do it sooner. Are you in the right vehicle to get you to your desired destination? That could mean finding the right upline, the right mentor, or just the right people in your community or industry. People are always the fastest way forward. If you find the right partners, the right relationships—they'll take you to places you couldn't have reached on your own. That's what I always tell people: it's always about people. It always comes down to relationships.

EMILY

Looking back, one of the biggest things I wish I had done earlier was to get clear on our end game—and then give myself permission to act boldly on it. In some ways, we were starting to gain clarity; we just hadn't taken the time to step back and define it fully. Eventually, we did. We paused, had honest conversations, and really thought about what our end game was. Once we did that, everything became so much clearer. And I have to say—Chase mentioning being bolder? That made me laugh. I definitely tend to play the balancing role in our relationship, but I really admire that quality in him. And, honestly, I think he's right. It takes a lot of courage to jump into something that feels uncomfortable—or even unsafe at first. Big risks are part of doing big things.

I remember being on maternity leave with our second daughter. That was when we started having real conversations about the brand, my role in the company, and how we could evolve both the internal insurance business and the larger vision. Leaving a career I had built over 16 years—at an organization I loved and that had treated me well—took real boldness. But looking back, I'm so grateful I made that move. It's been exciting to step into a whole new chapter. So, I want to echo Chase's point: boldness is essential. Yes, it's often a calculated risk—but more often than not, the stories behind championship teams involve people who pushed through, who showed grit, and who kept going through tough times. And that's what makes all the difference. So I think really leaning into that boldness is going to be key to getting you to where you really want to be and to be a true championship team.

CONCLUSION: THE DYNASTY MINDSET

First of all, I want to thank you—the reader—for choosing to read *Dynasty*. I truly hope you can feel the passion I have for teaching, leading, developing, and coaching agents and agencies across the country.

This book is really a culmination of the past ten years. It's filled with both successes and failures. My hope is that you walk away with valuable insights and a clear blueprint for breaking through whatever ceiling you're facing. I challenge you to ask yourself, *"Am I in the appropriate vehicle to get me to my desired destination?"* One thing I always say is that to be different, you need to BE DIFFERENT. Sometimes that means exploring new relationships and partnerships. Sometimes it means you need to get your butt in gear. The solution is always a YOU or WHO. Either YOU are the problem, or you haven't found the right WHO. If you think we could be the right WHO for you, let's jump on a call. I love talking to new agents each week, understanding their goals and vision, and truly developing a road map to get from A to B.

And ultimately, I would love to see you in The Coach's Office—

our twelve-month flagship program. That program is designed to walk you through every stage of your insurance agency journey—to improve it, optimize it, and help you reach the next level you've been working toward. We offer events, training, masterminds—whatever you need, there's an entry point for you. I can't wait to grow with you and hope to see you somewhere along the way.

Lastly, as I stated at the beginning of the book, I want to make sure you know... My promise to you: if you show up for me, I will show up for you—and I will not let you lose.

Innovate. Collaborate. WIN.

THANK YOU FOR READING DYNASTY!

BOOK YOUR FREE STRATEGY CALL WITH COACHG

As a thank-you for reading Dynasty, we'd love to offer you a complimentary call with our team. Whether you're an agent, agency owner, or just someone ready to play bigger— we'll help you get clear on your next move.

Scan the QR code to schedule your call.
This isn't a sales pitch. It's a strategy session.

We'll talk through where you are, where you want to go, and how COACHG can help you optimize, amplify, and scale— just like we've done for hundreds of others.

You've got the playbook. Now let's run the play.

I appreciate your interest in my book and value your feedback as it helps me improve future versions of this book. I would appreciate it if you could leave your invaluable review on Amazon.com with your feedback. Thank you!

www.ingramcontent.com/pod-product-compliance
Lightning Source LLC
LaVergne TN
LVHW052235110526
838202LV00109B/2636/J